THE CREDO

of

THE COMMONER

THE CREDO OF THE COMMONER

William Jennings Bryan

material selected by

William Jennings Bryan, Jr.

edited by

Franklin Modisett

printed at

Occidental College
Los Angeles

1968

Commemorative Edition

TABLE OF CONTENTS

DEDICATION   i

INTRODUCTION   iv

   I. ANCESTRY   1

  II. BASIC PRINCIPLES   6

 III. MEMORIES OF YOUTH   22

  IV. PUBLIC SPEAKING   28

   V. RELIGIOUS BELIEFS   33

  VI. DEFINITION OF DEMOCRACY   40

 VII. OPINIONS OF DOMESTIC ISSUES   53

       Equality
       Trusts
       Labor
       Income Tax
       Direct Vote of Senator
       One-Term Presidency
       Universal Suffrage
       Bimetallism
       Racial Attitude

VIII. OPINIONS ON FOREIGN ISSUES   75

       Tariff
       Imperialism
       Philippines
       Boers
       India
       International Arbitration

  IX. CREDO FOR DEMOCRATIC PARTY   92

   X. POLITICAL LIFE   102

  XI. FRIENDS' APPRAISALS   111

       POSTSCRIPT   119

       APPENDIXES   122

       A. Charles F. Horner's remembrance of Bryan
           as a Chautauqua speaker.
       B. William Jennings Bryan Jr.'s memorial speech

       INDEX

To simplify the citations after each excerpt, shortened titles have been used. The short form and the complete bibliographical information are listed below.

Memoirs	<u>The Memoirs of William Jennings Bryan</u>, by himself and his wife, Mary Baird Bryan, Philadelphia, Chicago, The John C. Winston Co., 1925.
Commoner	<u>The Commoner Condensed</u>, by William Jennings Bryan, New York, The Abbey Press, c. 1902-1907.
Life and Speeches	<u>Life and Speeches of William Jennings Bryan</u>, pamphlet, J. S. Ogilvie publishing house, 57 Rose St., New York, 1901.
Speeches	<u>Speeches of William Jennings Bryan</u>, rev. and arranged by himself, with a biographical introduction by Mary Baird Bryan, his wife; New York and London, Funk and Wagnalls, 1909, 1911, 1913.
Under Other Flags	<u>Under Other Flags</u>, travels, lectures, speeches; by William Jennings Bryan, Lincoln, Nebraska, the Woodruff-Collins Printing Company, 1904.
Old World	<u>The Old World and its Ways</u>, by William Jennings Bryan, describing a tour around the world and journeys through Europe, St. Louis, The Thompson publishing company, 1907.
The First Battle	<u>The First Battle</u>. A story of the campaign of 1896, by William Jennings Bryan, together with a collection of his speeches and a biographical sketch by his wife; Chicago, W. B. Conkey company, 1896.
Williams	<u>William Jennings Bryan</u>, by Wayne C. Williams, G. P. Putnam's Sons, New York, 1936.

DEDICATION

For more than 30 years, William Jennings Bryan was a dominant figure in American political life. Although he was twice elected to Congress as a Democrat and three times was the nominee of the Democratic Party for President of the United States, strictly partisan politics was actually a relatively small part of his public life.

His life was dedicated to public service, and he was a tireless crusader for every reform he felt was necessary to strengthen our government, protect the liberties and freedoms of the common people and advance their general welfare.

He was a unique personality--dynamic, courageous, and guided by the highest ideals--a man who believed that service was God's purpose in creating man, and that all political and social problems could be solved by the application of Christian principles.

His crusades were an altogether personal work, carried on at his own expense, without organization backing, or subsidies, or foundation grants--a fact that has been little understood by his biographers.

His newspaper, The Commoner, was not published for profit. It was a means to carry his views to literally hundreds of thousands of followers in all parts of the country. It was not uncommon for him to send out three or four hundred thousand personal letters upon some issue he felt was especially important.*

From his earliest days in Congress, he was in great demand in all parts of the country as a public speaker. Spending several months each year on the lecture platform enabled him to earn his livelihood and the funds to carry on his personal crusades.

Shortly before his death, he estimated that in each year after he left Congress in 1894, he had delivered at least 200 lectures while traveling a distance more than once around the world. This figure does not take into account the much greater number of speeches he made without compensation in connection with his public work.

He pioneered in advocating political reforms that were decades ahead of his time, and few men in American public life ever lived to see so many of their ideas and reforms accepted by the people at large and written into the fundamental law of the land. Among these, to mention a few, were the direct election of senators by the people, the income tax, the regulation of interstate commerce, the anti-trust laws, the guaranty of bank deposits, the Initiative and Referendum, woman's suffrage, and a government old age pension system similar to Social Security.

There were no radios and TV's in his day to carry his voice to an unseen audience. For thirty-five years he was constantly before the people, and there is no doubt that he met and spoke face to face with more of the American people than any other man in history.

Nor is it likely that any other man in public life kept personal contact with so many people for so many years. There was scarcely a county in any state where he did not have contact with personal friends.

He had in his personality an indefinable quality that bound people to him with a feeling much deeper than mere admiration. It was a bond of personal affection that is rarely found in public or private life. Indeed, to me,

* Letters in Occidental College Collection

the most remarkable attribute that Mr. Bryan possessed, was his ability to inspire in a multitude of followers the same faith and devotion that he felt for his fellow man.

It is not surprising, then, that so many biographies of William Jennings Bryan have been written and are still being written, and that historians and scholars continue to study and write of his life.

Most of the early biographies were written in the heat of political campaigns, and they dealt primarily with the issues of those campaigns and whether Bryan was right or wrong in the policies he advocated. They were, for the most part, biased for or against him, depending on the views of the writer.

However, they all have one thing in common, and that is their failure to adequately portray his unique personality and traits of character, not as a politician, but as a dedicated humanitarian and disciple of the social gospel.

For this reason, a few years ago, I determined to write a different kind of biography--one written for the sole purpose of revealing the true character and personality of a great and unusual man, and in which I proposed to limit any reference to political campaigns to the issues and statements that reflected his personality and character.

I felt that these traits of character could best be shown by quoting from his ideals and principles, as expressed in his own speeches and writings.

To this end, I began a review of my personal recollections from thirty-five years of close association with him, and our personal correspondence. I began a careful re-reading of his published books, his lectures, the editorials in his newspaper, The Commoner, articles, and other writings that were available to me.

This study continued for more than two years, and countless passages were earmarked for future reference, while many hundreds of quotations were immediately selected and reduced to writing. In each case, the source of the quotation was noted. These quotations will form the bulk of the material that will appear on the following pages.

I have quoted extensively from Mr. Bryan's memoirs containing his description of his childhood and early education, as these passages throw much light upon the foundations of his character.

At the Nebraska State Centennial Celebration of the day of his birth, held at Lincoln, Nebraska, March 19, 1960, I made a talk about his personality. A copy of this address is included herein for the personal recollections it contains.

The only other extraneous material included in this work is a wonderful description of Mr. Bryan's personality as a lecturer on the Chautauqua platform from Charles F. Horner's book, Strike the Tents.

Horner arranged Mr. Bryan's lectures for more than eighteen years, traveled with him on the lecture circuits, and heard and watched him speak literally thousands of times. I consider it the finest exposition of Mr. Bryan's speaking personality and his rapport with his audience that has ever been written. I am deeply indebted to Horner for permission to quote extensively from his book.

Some two years ago, failing eyesight forced me to abandon my plans, and while surgery has restored some vision, further research and the completion of the biography I had hoped to write are no longer possible.

However, I feel that this compilation of research materials will provide a unique and valuable source of information for future students and scholars.

The quotations were all gleaned from my father's writings by one who was his constant companion for more than thirty years and knew his personality and character first hand, and certainly there is no other single source where so many of his own words, expressing his ideals and beliefs, and revealing his personality and character, can be found.

I am compiling these materials, and making them available to future students and scholars, as my personal memorial to my father, whom I revere as the finest Christian character I have ever known.

I want to express my deep appreciation to Occidental college and to Tyrus G. Harmsen, its Librarian, and to Noah Franklin Modisett, for their fine assistance in editing and arranging these materials and making the distribution of this publication possible.

William Jennings Bryan, Jr.
Laguna Beach, California
1968

INTRODUCTION

The time is coming for a reevaluation of William Jennings Bryan. Many Americans probably envision him as an old-fashioned, rotund, oratorical fundamentalist. Their most durable impression was understandably fostered by the portrayals of him in the play and movie <u>Inherit the Wind</u>. Against the sympathetically presented Charles Darrow, Bryan seems to be a rock-ribbed villain who reveres the old and fears the new.

No impression could be further from the truth. Too many important factors are ignored or forgotten in this appraisal. First, it ignores that Bryan was in the month of his death at the Scopes trial, whereas his most productive period was twenty to thirty years earlier. Second, it mistakenly judges that he was protesting the teaching of evolution as a theory, whereas he merely objected to teaching it as a law. Third, it overlooks the record of what he said and did during the other thirty-four years of his public life.

William Jennings Bryan espoused more political, economic, and social reforms than any other candidate of his time. Some of his ideas have only recently become practice. He consistently supported: direct primaries, women's suffrage, direct election of senators, a single term for the President, no lame-duck Congress, the initiative, referendum, and recall, tariff reduction, graduated income tax, enforcement of the Sherman Anti-Trust Act, publication of campaign contributions, guaranteed bank deposits, eight-hour day, licensed corporations, government by injunction, independence for the Philippines, conservation of resources, and international arbitration.

To help refocus our view, the intent of this book is to present the essence of Bryan's writings and character as seen by his closest observer, William Jennings Bryan, Jr. It has been my privilege to work with the latter in selecting, arranging and editing the most revealing and pertinent lines from his father's books. If these excerpts conjure up a vision of a strong-willed, deeply-principled, devoutly-religious, warmly-human, far-sighted political reformer, we will have accomplished our purpose.

I thank Tyrus Harmsen for his kindness, Helen Brammer for her competence, and William Jennings Bryan, Jr. for his patience.

Franklin Modisett
Los Angeles   1968

CHAPTER

I

ANCESTRY

Geneology

We know nothing of the parents, brothers, or sisters of William Bryan, my great-grandfather, and therefore have been unable to answer a multitude of questions which have been asked from time to time, the most persistent being whether our ancestor was related to the wife of Daniel Boone, whose maiden name was Bryan. William Bryan had three sons, Aquilla, James, and John. Aquilla Bryan, the oldest of the three sons, left Sperryville before or soon after my father's birth, to try his fortune in the Great West which was then inviting adventurers. When he reached the Ohio River the water was so high that instead of descending the river as he had intended, he crossed into Ohio and then waited for the waters to subside. That is the last knowledge we have of him that is authentic.

James, the second son, went to Kentucky and located at Glasgow, where some of the family still reside.

John Bryan, my father's father, moved from his birthplace to Point Pleasant in what is now West Virginia. There my father spent part of his boyhood, but his mother died when he was twelve and his father when he was fourteen years old and Silas was entrusted to the care of different members of the family. His oldest brother, William Bryan, to whom I am indebted for the first part of my name, located on a farm near Troy, Missouri, where some of his descendents still live. Russell Bryan, his younger brother, located at Salem, where he raised a numerous family. His children were among my earliest playmates and most beloved companions.

John Bryan, my grandfather, was married to Nancy Lillard, a member of an English family. They lived in Culpeper County. This family was quite large and made up of men and women of character and virtue.

Memoirs, pp. 20-21.

Early Work and Education of Silas Lillard Bryan

As none of the brothers or sisters of my father were rich, he had the advantage of having to work. I do not know that this spur of necessity was absolutely necessary, but it is no disadvantage and it is possibly the best insurance against the influences that sap the energies and industry of young men. He had caught from some one the ambition to learn and though he had to work his way through school, he went further than any of his brothers or sisters in the pursuit of learning. When he was far enough advanced to teach, he earned, by teaching, the money necessary to complete his college course, which was taken at McKendree College, Lebanon, Illinois. He had intended to attend a Baptist college, but for some reason changed his plans and entered the Methodist college above named. He took the classical course, graduating in 1849, and was always an enthusiastic believer in classical education for the young. He was a good student and interested also in the literary societies.

As father did not graduate until he was twenty-seven, he was one of the older students, although the age of graduation was probably older then than now.

Memoirs, p. 22.

Silas Bryan's Religious Attitude

Father was a very devout Christian. Just when he joined the Church I do not know, but it was probably at an early age. There came a day, however, when he was a young man, when religion took a very strong hold upon him and held him and became a controlling influence in his life. As a young man he was fond of fun and took delight in the frivolities of his day. One night as he went to a party he took cold and the cold developed into pneumonia. His condition finally became so critical that the attending physician thought it wise to inform him that, while his life was not despaired of, it would be the part of wisdom for him to make such provision for the future as he might think best. When the physician retired, father prayed as he had never prayed before and promised the Heavenly Father that if restored to health he would pray three times a day as long as he lived. He was restored to health and kept the promise.

Memoirs, p. 23.

Father's Religious Influence on William Jennings Bryan

This thrice-a-day prayer is the basis upon which numerous elaborations have been built. After my nomination for the Presidency a great many stories were told, differing in detail but all emphasizing the devotional side of my father's life. One story was that he opened court with prayer. Another, that he always prayed for guidance before rendering a decision. The first was not true, but knowing as I do his dependence upon God for guidance, I have no doubt that he invoked aid when entering upon anything important. I may add that my father's attitude on spiritual matters made a very deep impression upon me. There was a family altar in our house and the children were brought up according to the strictest views in religious matters, and my gratitude for such a home environment increased with the years. I shall be happy if my children feel toward me in mature life as I feel toward my father; if they revere my name as I revere my father's name and feel as deeply indebted to me for whatever there is in me of good.

Memoirs, pp. 24-25.

Silas Bryan's Public Life

After graduation at the age of twenty-seven, my father moved to Salem, the county seat of Marion County, Illinois, in which two of his sisters lived. At the age of twenty-nine he was admitted to the bar and about the same time or possibly a little earlier was elected superintendent of schools of that county. He began the practice of law in 1851 and in 1852 was elected to the Senate of the State of Illinois, where he served for eight years. He soon became prominent at the bar, and prominent also as a public speaker. In 1860, at the age of thirty-eight, he was elected a judge of the Circuit that included about half a dozen counties and was re-elected in 1866, serving until 1872.

In 1869 he was elected a member of the Constitutional Convention of Illinois and assisted in the drafting of that constitution. After his death I found in his library two volumes containing a record of the proceedings of the Constitutional Convention. On the fly-leaf of the first volume I found a dedication of the books to myself. I immediately examined it, desiring to see what part he took, and was interested to find that at the very beginning of the session he introduced a resolution which reads as follows:

> "Resolved, By the Convention: First - That all officers to be provided for in the new Constitution in the executive, legislative, and judicial departments, shall be elected by the people. Second - That the compensation to be allowed for official service in the several departments of the government shall be fixed in the Constitution, and shall not be increased or lessened by the legislative department."

It interested me to know that he shared Jefferson's confidence in the capacity of the people for self-government as well as in their right to self-government. He believed in entrusting them with their own affairs, as this resolution indicated. I have credited him with a definite influence in the shaping of my religious views; I am also indebted to him for the trend of my views on some fundamental questions of government, and have seen no reason to depart from the lines he marked out.

Memoirs, pp. 24-25.

Mariah Elizabeth Jennings

Mother was born on May 24th, 1834, at Walnut Hill, a rural community near Centralia, Marion County, Illinois. She was reared in the country and attended the public school in the neighborhood. She was married at the age of eighteen (1852) and began housekeeping in the home on Broadway, about halfway between the public square and the railroad. Father helped to hew out the timbers and build their house. The style of it was that which was customary in that day. It had a room on each side of a short central hall, with two rooms upstairs over these lower rooms and a dining room and kitchen in the rear. In this house, the first six children were born.

Memoirs, p. 27.

Effect of Mother on Character

My father being absent at court a considerable portion of the time, the burden of directing the family affairs and taking full control of the children fell upon her (mother). Every duty was faithfully discharged. As I look back upon those early days, I cannot recall a single word that she ever said or a single act of hers that to me seems worthy of criticism. I feel that she was as nearly a perfect wife and mother as one could be. When father died, her oldest child was twenty-two, I was twenty, and the youngest child was ten. She assumed with courage the double responsibility of being to the children both mother and father. She survived my father sixteen years and lived to see her children grown, settled, and successful in life, and was revered by all of them. As a mother, she had one advantage that can hardly be overestimated. Her husband set an example in word and conduct that she could always invoke in the training of the children. Not in a single matter was it necessary to warn the children against following their father's example. Thus the memory of the two is entwined as if of a single character, so much alike were they in all that contributed to character building.

Memoirs, pp. 29-30.

Father's Beliefs of Sources of Happiness

Later in reading over an address delivered by father to the grand jury as he left the bench after a term of twelve years service as circuit judge, I find this, which you will pardon me for quoting. "I have not grown rich from the spoils of office. During the whole term of twelve years I have received not more than a living. I have nevertheless succeeded reasonably well in the affairs of life and have of the world's goods a reasonable competency, but it has not come to me from office. It has been the result of rigid economy, long and patient professional labor, and the sweat of the face in agricultual pur- suits, aided and supported by Heaven's greatest bestowment - an affectionate, confiding and prudential companion - and finally, gentlemen of the jury, I add that the experience of public life has tended to confirm in me the convictions of my early education - that the more we conform our lives and actions, both in private and public relations, to the demands of honor, truth, sincerity, justice and christianity, the greater will be our happiness and prosperity, and the better we shall enjoy this present world, and the broader will be our foundation for the enjoyment of the world to come."
Such is the example set me by my venerated father.

Memoirs, p. 242.

Value of Good Ancestors

Ancestry counts. We inherit more than we ourselves can add. It means much to be borne of a race with centuries of civilization back of it. Blood, if it be good, inspires one to great effort - if it be bad it may paralyze ambition and fix the boundary to one's possibilitites. I am speaking of the rule, not of the rare exceptions; many have become degenerate in spite of inheriting the stimulus to better things, and a few have, to a degree, overcome handicaps of their life and early environment.

If one is tempted to boast that he is self-made, a few reflections will puncture his pride. Let him analyze himself, separate all that has come to him into three factors: one representing that which has come to him by inheritance; another representing that which has entered his life through environment; the third representing what he can fairly credit to himself - that which is not based upon either inheritance or environment - and the third factor will not be large enough to flatter his vanity.

The child comes into the world without its own volition, containing within himself capacities and weaknesses for which he is in no way responsible; he finds himself in an environment which he did not choose and cannot control. His first impressions come to him with breath and his life is largely moulded for him before he has intelligence to choose or standards by which to measure effort.

It is a consciousness of the helplessness of the new-born babe and of his dependence upon an unknown past and upon surroundings that he cannot comprehend that makes me increasingly grateful for the parentage with which the Heavenly Father blessed me and for the home in which my life began.

Memoirs, pp. 18-19.

CHAPTER

II

BASIC PRINCIPLES

Importance of Principles

If one attempted to draw a tree through a narrow gate by taking hold of one of the branches he would find that the other branches would spread out so that he could not get the tree through the gate, but that if he would take the stem or trunk of the tree and pull that through first, then he would have no difficulty. I often think of that illustration. A study of the details without a knowledge of the principles involved is only confusing, but a study of principles makes the details plain.

Life and Speeches, p. 319.

Decisions Based on Moral Principle

I do not like to discuss a question without reaching down to the moral principle upon which it rests, for the older I grow the more convinced I am that there is no great question that is not in its essence a moral question. No question is ever settled until the justice or injustice of the question is determined, and in no way can you appeal to the people with such hope of success as in appealing to the conscience, to the moral sense of the people.

Commoner, Vol VI, p. 153.

Basis of Bryan's Political Philosophy

With the orator and the statesman, however, breadth of sympathy is indispensable. We labor for those whom we love; no other motive is sufficient to direct a large life and nothing begets love but love itself. They love him because he first loved them can be said of all who have been loved by the people. Only when orators and statesmen devote themselves unselfishly to the welfare of the whole people do they link themselves to those eternal forces which give assurance of permanent progress. They enter into partnership with nature, as it were, and grow with the cause which they aid.

Memoirs, p. 513.

Moral Sense in Politics

No cause can prosper permanently that does not appeal to the moral sense of the country, and the moral sense of the country is now being awakened to the importance of purifying politics.

Commoner, Vol V, p. 62.

The Value of an Ideal

If, I repeat, a man measures life by what others do for him, he is apt to be disappointed, but if he measures life by what he does for others, there is no time for despair. If he measures life by its accumulations, these usually fall short of his expectations, but if he measures life by the contribution which he makes to the sum of human happiness, his only disappointment is in not finding time to do all that his heart prompts him to do. Whether he spends his time trying to absorb from the world, only to have the burden of life grow daily heavier, or spends his time in an effort to accomplish something of real value to the race, depends upon his ideal.

> Speeches, Vol II, p. 236, "The Value of an Ideal", lecture delivered at numerous Chautauquas and College meetings beginning in 1901.

Service Repays Debt to Ancestors

We have received so much from the generations past and from those about us that, instead of boasting of what we have done, we ought to learn humility and be content if at the end of life we can look back over the years and be assured that we have given to the world a service equal to that which we have received.

> Speeches, Vol II, p. 247.

Need for Ideals

Not only must the individual have an ideal, but we must have ideals as groups of individuals and in every department of life. We have our domestic ideals. Whether a marriage is happy or not depends not so much upon the size of the house or the amount of the income, as upon the ideals with which the parties enter marriage. If two people contract marriage like some people trade horses - each one trying to get the better of the bargain - it is not certain that the marriage will be a happy one. In fact, the man who cheats in a horse trade has at least one advantage over the man who cheats in matrimony. The man who cheats in a horse trade may console himself with the thought that he may never see again the person whom he has cheated. Not so fortunate is the man who cheats in marriage. He not only sees daily the person whom he has cheated, but he is sometimes reminded of it - and it is just as bad if the cheating is done by the other side.

There is an American ideal of domestic life. When two persons, drawn together by the indissoluble ties of love, enter marriage, each one contributing a full part and both ready to share life's struggles and trials as well as its victories and its joys - when these mutually helpful and mutually forebearing, start out to build an American home it ought to be the fittest earthly type of heaven.

> Speeches, Vol II, pp. 248-249.

Highest Ideal

There is this difference between the ideal and other things of value, namely, that an ideal cannot be patented or copyrighted. We often see things that we cannot hope to possess, but there is no ideal, however high, that cannot be ours if we desire it. The highest ideal of human life that this world has ever known was that furnished by the life of the Man of Galilee, but it was an ideal within the comprehension of the fishermen of his day, and the Bible says of Him that the common people heard Him gladly. So with a high party ideal. It can be comprehended by all the members of the party, and it can be adopted by every party. If we can fight out political battles upon this plane there is no humiliation about defeat. I have passed through two presidential campaigns, and many have rejoiced over my defeats, but if events prove that my defeats have been good for this country, I shall rejoice over them myself more than any opponent has rejoiced. And when I say this I am not unselfish, for it is better for me that my political opponents should bring good to my country than that I should by any mistake of mine bring evil.

Speeches, Vol II, p. 258.

All Classes May Serve

The ideal dominates the life, determines the character, and fires a man's place among his fellows. I have known laboring men who, working for wages, have been able to support themselves, acquire a library and become acquainted with the philosophers, orators and historians of the world, and many of them have laid aside enough to gratify their ambition for a college course. What enables them to resist temptation and press forward to the consumation of a high purpose? It is their ideal of life. As I have gone through the country I have found here and there young men - sometimes the sons of farmers, sometimes the sons of mechanics, sometimes the sons of merchants, sometimes the sons of professional men - young men who have one characteristic in common, namely, that they have been preparing for service.

Speeches, Vol II, pp. 240-241.

One's Ideals Influences Others

As our lives are built upon ideals, the greatest service which can be rendered to one is to raise his ideals and give him a broader view of life. A parent does this by example and by daily precept; the teacher in the pulpit and in the school-room does the same and the editor is not without responsibility. Everyone, in fact, has some influence on someone and that influence ought to be exerted for good. What is the value of an ideal? Sometimes it may make the difference between success and failure - between happiness and despair.

Commoner, Vol I, p. 351.

Ideal Should be Unattainable

I know, therefore, of no greater service that my country can render to the world than to furnish to the world the highest ideal that the world has known. That ideal must be so far above us that it will keep us looking upward all our lives, and so far in advance of us that we shall never overtake it. I know of no better illustration of an ideal life than the living spring, pouring forth constantly of that which refreshes and invigorates - no better illustration of a worthless life than the stagnant pool which receives contribution from all the land around and gives forth nothing.

Speeches, Vol II, p. 202.

Value of Great Service

So almost limitless are the possibilities of service in this age that I am not willing to fix a maximum to the sum a man can honestly and legitimately earn.

Not only do I believe that a man can earn five hundred million, but I believe that men have earned it. I believe that Thomas Jefferson earned more than five hundred millions. The service that he rendered to the world was of such great value that he collected for it five hundred millions of dollars, he would not have been overpaid. I believe that Abraham Lincoln earned more than five hundred millions, and I could go back through history and give you the name of man after man who rendered a service so large as to entitle him to collect more than five hundred million from society, but if I presented a list containing the name of every man, who, since time began, earned such an enormous sum, one thing would be true of all of them, namely; that in not a single case did the man collect the full amount. The men who have earned five million dollars have been so busy earning it that they have not had time to collect it; and the men who have collected five hundred million have been so busy collecting it that they have not had time to earn it.

Speeches, Vol II, pp. 342-343. "The Price of a Soul", abstract of address delivered first at Northwestern Law School Banquet in Chicago, then as Commencement Oration Pierce School in Philadelphia, and in 1909 extended into a lecture.

Giving to Others

Giving ought not to be confined to the rich; it is as necessary to moral growth as exercise is to the body. Selfishness leads one to spend money for himself - stingyness leads one to refuse to spend even on himself, while generosity leads one to share his means with benevolences which appeal to him.

Every heart should attach itself in some definite way to the world's needs, and without waiting for great wealth or for death, set aside a part of each year's income for the happiness and health of those less fortunate.

"Others"is the word that marks the crossing of the boundaries of selfishness and man's entrance into fellowship with the outer world.

Commoner, Vol IV, p. 381.

Good Character

Good character in the individual is nothing more than the habitual right-eousness. No man can establish a character worth having if he is guided in each business transaction solely by the amount that he can make. He must be guided by rules that compel him to deal justly with his fellows.

Commoner, Vol IV, p. 437.

Effect of Loving Heart

What can a human being do? You can measure the influence that one body can exert on another; you can estimate the influence that one mind can exercise over another; but no human being can estimate the influence that one heart can exert on the heart of the human race. One heart full of love, one heart willing to do and dare, kindles enthusiasm and makes the impossible possible.

Commoner, Vol VI, p. 160.

Heart Over Mind

We have overestimated, I think, the relative importance of the mind, and underestimated the relative importance of the heart in the shaping of human happiness. When I say this do not think that I lack interest in Education. I am an enthusiast on the subject of education. I am anxious that every boy and girl in this land shall be educated. Nothing made me more indignant in 1896 than the statement of an eminent divine who declared that the farmer's sons were being educated so much that they were getting dissatisfied with the position that God intended them to fill. God never made any man wise enough to say in advance what position your boy or my boy was intended to fill. God never made any man wise enough to draw a line and say that the children on one side should be educated and the children on the other side should be neglected. I want my children educated, but I want my neighbor's children educated also, so that if my children lack wisdom they may have the benefit of the wisdom of my neighbor's children. But as enthusiastic as I am on the subject of education, I repeat that I think we have boasted too much of what the mind has done, and not sufficiently considered what the heart can do. We talk of the inventions of genius, and they have indeed been great. We are amazed to think that a man can stand by the side of the telegraph instrument and by means of the electric current talk with people ten thousand miles away, but if that achievement is wonderful, the achievements of the heart are still more wonderful. The

heart that is full of love for its fellows, the heart that yearns to do some
great good, the heart that puts into operation some movement for the uplifting
of the human race, that heart will speak to hearts that will beat ten thousand
years after all our hearts are still. That is more wonderful than talking to
people ten thousand miles away.

Under Other Flags, pp. 260-261.

Lifelong Student

"I address you as fellow students, for I am also a student. I began
studying when I was young - younger than any of you here. I have studied ever
since, and I hope that I will not graduate from study until my life closes. .
All life is a school to those who improve it as they ought. None of us are
too old to learn. None of us know all that can be known, and no one is so
humble that he cannot teach others something.

The receptive mind is characteristic of the student, and I would rather
talk to students than to any other class of people. I talk to them in my own
country, and I am glad to talk to them in every country which I have the good
fortune to visit.

The student is passing through the springtime of life. In the spring
we sow the seed - it is the time of year when the sowing gives the greatest
promise of a crop; so that when you leave a thought with a student it grows
and develops.

In the first place, let me say to you that while things seem strange to
a visitor, whether he visits this land or any other land - while these differences first attract attention, yet after all we are much alike. If you look
at the eye of the human being you find that it may have a color that is distinctly its own, and you begin to classify eyes. Some will have blue eyes,
some will have brown eyes, some will have black eyes, but no matter what the
color of the eye is, it looks out upon the same landscape and sees the same
things. And so we may differ in appearance or in features, we may differ in
size, we may differ in dress, but after all we are human beings and we have
the same impulses and the same purposes.

I say however much we differ in appearance, in dress, in custom, when
you come to know people you find that they are very much alike, and when you
can touch you find that the heart of man differs less than the face or even
the mind. And so I am sure that if I speak from my heart I can speak to
the heart of those who listen to me.

...If any person thinks that education is merely given to him in order
to enable him to get all possible advantage over other people, then it is
doing him as much good as it ought to do. But if he understands that it is
given him in order to make him more useful and helpful, and to help him to
do a larger work for mankind, then he cannot have too much education.

And as we get older, things that seem very important to us when young
seem less so. Some spend their lives trying to make money, to surround themselves with riches; others seek to gain high position; but as they get older
they find that their place in history will be determined, not by what people

have done for them, but by what they have done for the people."

Commoner, Vol VI, p. 14. From an account in the _Japanese Times_ of Tokyo of Bryan's speech at Wasada University. It is typical of his talks to students at many different places during his trip around the world.

Value of Education and Service

No one is quite above the level of the brute who considers mere wealth in estimating success in individual or national life. If food and physical development are all that one wants the beasts of the fields may surpass him; if fine apparel is man's chief desire the flowers and birds outstrip him; if his only thought is of himself, and if he only labors to gratify himself, he puts himself in the class with the vulture and the glutton. He only values life as he should who recognizes it as a responsibility no less than a privilege and strives to measure up to his opportunities. If his ideals are lofty enough to keep his face turned upward to the very end of life and his principles are strong enough to keep him always moving forward he will find the very highest education and the most extensive knowledge insufficient to gratify his ambition to serve.

Commoner, Vol II, p. 169.

What is Man?

The Psalmist asks of Jehovah, "What is man, that thou art mindful of him, and the son of man, that thou visitest him?" And answering his own question he adds: "For thou has made him a little lower than the angels, and has crowned him with glory and honor."

Commoner, Vol V, pp. 168-169.

Physical Moderation

Man shares with the animal a physical nature - he has a body, the citadel of the mind, the temporary tenement of the soul. It is necessary that this link in the endless chain that connects the generations past with the generations yet to come shall be made as strong as conditions, heredity and environment will permit. Infinitely varied are the physical capabilities bequeathed to us by our ancestors. Some of us are heirs to virtuous estates with which no courts can interfere; some of us bear in our bodies the evidence of ancestral sins and are living proof of the fact that the iniquities of the parents are visited upon the children. All of us inherit both the weaknesses and elements of strength. It is within our power to conserve and to increase the strength that has come down to us, and it is also within our power to dissipate the physical fortune which we have received. Nothing but a proper conception of the creature's stewardship under the Creator can protect the individual from the rust of inaction, the wear of excess and the waste that arises from a perverted use of the powers of the body.

Commoner, Vol V, pp. 169-170.

Difference Between Man and Brute

Man is distinguished from the brute in that the latter merely eats and sleeps and dies, while man is endowed by the Creator with infinite Possibilities. Liberty is necessary for the realization of man's possibilities. His conscience must be left free that he may fix for himself the relation between himself and his God. His mind must be left free that he may devise and plan for himself, for his family and for his fellows. His speech must be free that he may give to the world the results of his investigations and present to others the ideal which he is trying to realize in his work. His pen must be free that he may scatter seed thoughts to the uttermost parts of the earth and leave to posterity a record of his work. He finds in government the cheapest, as well as the surest, protection of this liberty, to be, to think, to speak, to act.

Speeches, Vol II, p. 177.

Ages of Man

Man is the miracle of miracles. What unfathomed possibilities are wrapped within the swaddling clothes that enfold an infant! Who can measure a child's influence for weal or woe? Before it can lisp a word, it has brought to one woman the sweet consciousness of motherhood, and it has given to one man the added strength that comes with a sense of responsibility. Before its tiny hands can lift a feather's weight, they have drawn two hearts closer together and its innocent prattle echoes through two lives. Every day that child in its growth touches and changes someone; not a year in all its history but that it leaves an impress upon the race. Its smiles, its tears, its joys, its sorrows - all are garnered up, and when that child reaches the age of fifteen or sixteen and the parents send it to college they entrust this priceless creature to the care of teachers. What do they do with it? How do you deal with it? Train it in the sciences? Train it in the languages? It is not sufficient that the child shall know how old the earth is, how far the stars are apart, or the forces that attract or repel each other. There is something more important to that child than any or all of these - it is to know how to live, and how can that child know how to live unless it knows that it is linked by indissoluble ties to every other human being? Great is the responsibility of the college! The college ought to send forth, not simply scholars, but men and women prepared to do great work.

Commoner, Vol V, pp.434-435.

Each Man a Part of All

If civilization can be defined - and I know of no better definition - as the harmonious development of the human race, physically, mentally and morally, then each individual, whether his influence is perceptable or not, raises the level of the civilization of his age just in proportion as he contributes to world's work a body, a mind and a heart capable of maximum effort. No one lives unto himself or dies unto himself. The tie that binds each human being to every other human being is one that can not be severed. We can not without shame invite a physical weakness that can be avoided or continue one which can be remedied. The burdens to be borne are great enough to tax the resources of all when service is rendered under the most favorable conditions; no one has a right to offer less than the best within his power.

Commoner, Vol V, p. 170

Power of Conscience

The conscience is the most potent force of which man has knowledge. Its decrees are more binding than statute law; its mandates are more imperative than the warrants of a king, and the invisible barriers which it raises are stronger than prison walls. There is no resisting the conscience when it is once aroused. To satisfy its demands men have faced death without a fear; in obedience to its promptings, and aglow with an all-pervading love, others have traversed oceans, buried themselves among strangers, and devoted their lives to the elevation of men and women to whom they were bound only by the primary tie which links each human being to every other.

Commoner, Vol V, pp. 156-157.

Power of Character

But there are those who have both influence through life and unending praises after death; there are those who have by their ability inspired the admiration of the people, and held it by the purity of their character. It is often remarked that some men have a name greater than their works will justify; the secret lies in the men themselves.

Life and Speeches, p. 29.

Slow Creation of Character

Character is the entity, the individuality of the person, shining from every window of the soul, either as a beam of purity, or as a clouded ray that betrays the impurity within. The contest between light and darkness, right and wrong, goes on; day by day, hour by hour, moment by moment, our characters are being formed, and this is the all important question which comes to us in accents ever growing fainter as we journey from the cradle to the grave "Shall those characters be good or bad."

Life and Speeches, p. 33.

Beginning of Evil

There is perhaps no more important lesson that young or old can learn than that evils are more easily resisted in the beginning than after they have been allowed to develop. Take, for instance, disobedience to parents. It usually begins in some small matter when the child feels that the parent has required an unnecessary thing, or refused to permit something that the child desires to do. If it were in an important matter the child would shrink from an act of disobedience, but it seems so small that the wish of the child triumphs over the will of the father or mother, and that act of disobedience becomes the precedent for others until disobedience is easier than obedience.

Disobedience usually leads to other offenses; untruthfulness, especially, is apt to follow in the wake of disobedience, being resorted to as a means of avoiding punishment or even reproof.

From disregard of parental authority it is an easy step to the disregard of the authority of government, and the disobedient child not unnaturally develops into the lawless citizen until finally the downward course leads to the door of some institution established for correction and reform. Disobedience to authority is more easily checked when it first begins to manifest itself than after the habit has grown strong by indulgence.

Commoner, Vol III, p. 297.

Daily Development of Character

But if each day we gather some new truths, plant ourselves more firmly upon principles which are eternal, guard every thought and action, that it may be pure, and conform our lives more nearly to that Perfect Model, we shall form a character that will be a fit background on which to paint the noblest deeds and the grandest intellectual and moral achievements - a character that cannot be concealed, but which will bring success in this life and form the best preparation for that which is beyond.

Life and Speeches, p. 30.

Democracy Mirror of the People

My friends, in this world people have just about as much of good as they deserve. At least, the best way to secure anything that is desirable is to first deserve that thing. If the people of this country want good laws they themselves must secure them. If the people want to repeal bad laws they alone have the power to do it. In a government like ours every year offers the citizen an opportunity to prove his love of country. Every year offers him an opportunity to manifest his patriotism.

Life and Speeches, pp. 316-317.

Morality Paramount in Government

My investigation has led me to believe that the moral element is not only important but paramount in government, and that the decay of nations has been due to a decay in the moral elements. A government is strong in proportion as it rests upon justice; it becomes weak in proportion as injustice is substituted for justice. . . . If the time ever comes when this nation shall turn downward and at last by its wreck and ruin furnish a warning to the nations that comes after it, it will be because of moral decay among the people and in our government. . . .

I will go further than that; I know of no moral principle that can be applied to one human being that cannot be applied - aye, that must not be applied - to eighty millions of human beings acting together as a nation. One of the great dangers of the present day is the tendency to limit and amend and qualify great moral principles. Let me illustrate. There is a commandment which reads: "Thou shalt not steal." That is the way we learned it. It is simple and plain and strong, but it is being amended to read, "Thou shalt not steal - on a small scale." If the larceny is on a large scale it is different. I am not revealing any secrets when I tell you that as a rule it is safer in this country to steal a million dollars than it is to steal a hundred dollars.

Under Other Flags, pp. 249-250-251.

Demagogue or Statesman

The difference between a demagogue and a statesman is that the former advocates what he thinks will be popular, regardless of the effect that it may ultimately have upon the people to whom he appeals; the statesman advocates what he believes to be the best for the country, regardless of the immediate effect which it may have upon himself. One is willing to sacrifice the permanent interests of others to advance his own temporary interests, while the other is willing to sacrifice his own temporary interests to advance the public welfare.

Commoner, Vol III, p. 158.

Die for Rights of Others

I appeal to you to meet these questions with the heroism that your ancestors displayed. If they were willing to die for their rights, are you not willing to respect the rights of others as well as to defend your own? There is something that is greater than dying for one's own rights. That is great, but I am looking for the time when there will be something greater yet, (a civilization beyond any that we have yet seen) a civilization in which the greatest citizen will be, not the man who will die in defense of his own rights, but the man who will die rather than trespass upon the rights of another.

Under Other Flags, p. 303.

Free Speech

Free speech is not consistent with military rule or carpetbag government. Men who exercise authority without responsibility to those whom they govern cannot tolerate criticism, and any suggestion of malfeasance or misfeasance becomes incendiary and dangerous. Human frailty makes public officials liable enough to err even though restrained by a free press and when that restraint is taken away the people have no protection whatever. There is a love of justice to be found in every human heart, and when justice is denied, those who are responsible for the denial never think it wise to have the matter discussed.

Commoner, Vol I, p. 390.

Faith

I have sometimes thought of preparing a speech on faith as a subject, for the older I grow the more I appreciate the influence of faith on one's conduct. Not only in the church is faith essential, but faith is necessary everywhere.

Commoner, Vol VI, p. 344.

Faith in Ourselves and Mankind

First - you must have faith in yourselves. Not that you should carry confidence in yourselves to the point of displaying egotism, and yet, egotism is not the worst possible fault. My father was wont to say that if a man had the big head, you could whittle it down, but that if he had the little head, there was no hope for him. If you have the big head others will help you reduce it, but if you have the little head, they cannot help you. You must believe that you can do things or you will not undertake them.

Those who lack faith attempt nothing and therefore cannot possibly succeed; those with great faith attempt the seemingly impossible and by attempting prove what man can do.

Second - have faith in mankind. The great fault of our scholarship is that it is not sufficiently sympathetic. It holds itself aloof from the struggling masses. It is too often cold and cynical. It is better to trust your fellowmen and be occasionally deceived than to be distrustful and live alone. Mankind deserves to be trusted. There is something good in every one, and that good responds to sympathy. If you speak to the multitude and they do not respond, do not despise them, but rather examine what you have said. If you speak from your heart, you will speak to their hearts, and they can tell very quickly whether you are interested in them or simply in your-self. The heart of mankind is sound; the sense of justice is universal.

Link yourselves in sympathy with our fellowmen; mingle with them; know them and you will trust them and they will trust you. If you are stronger than others, bear heavier loads; if you are more capable than others, show it by your willingness to perform a larger service.

Speeches, Vol II, p. 220.

Faith Generates Achievement

It is true today, and has been true through all history that "One with God shall chase a thousand, and two put ten thousand to flight."

If your preparation is complete so that you are conscious of your ability to do great things; if you have faith in your fellowmen and become a co-laborer with them in the raising of the general level of society; if you have faith in our form of government and seek to purge it of its imperfections so as to make it more and more acceptable to our own people and to the opprest of other nations; and if, in addition, you have faith in God and in the triumph of the right, no one can set limits to your achievements.

Speeches, Vol II; p. 336.

Faith in Democratic Ideas

In business faith is necessary, it is necessary to the farmer. He would not put in his crop in the spring if he had no faith in the autumn harvests. And so in politics faith is necessary. A man wouldn't labor if he had no faith in the triumph of his cause.

I have had faith in democratic ideas from the time I was a young man. My father left me a lesson before he was taken from us . . . and the lesson was this:

That I could afford to be in a minority, but that I could not afford to be in the wrong, for he said if I was in the minority and right I was apt some day to be in the majority, while if I was in the majority and wrong I would some day find myself in the minority.

It has been worth a great deal to me. I have had faith in the omnipotence
of truth and today I believe more firmly than ever in the final triumph of
every righteous cause.

It doesn't discourage me if defeat comes, for I know it takes time to brin
success to anything that is good.

Commoner, Vol VI, p. 345.

Food for Body, Mind and Heart

Let him feed his body with food convenient for it, remembering that food
is only useful in so far as it strengthens man for his work; let him train his
mind to search for the truth, remembering that his power to discern the truth
will increase with the effort to find it. Let him keep his heart diligently,
for 'out of it are the issues of life.' Let him recognize service as the
measure of greatness, and estimate life by its outgo rather than by its income. Let him to himself be true, 'and it follows as the night the day, he
cannot then be false to any man.'

Memoirs, p. 7.

Mystery of Creation

Did you ever raise a radish? You put a small black seed into the black
soil and in a little while you return to the garden and find the full-grown
radish. The top is green, the body white and almost transparent, and the skin
a delicate red or pink. What mysterious power reaches out and gathers from the
ground the particles which give it form and size and flavor? Whose is the invisible brush that transfers to the root, growing in darkness, the hues of the
summer sunset? If we were to refuse to eat anything until we could understand
the mystery of its creation we would die of starvation - but mystery, it seems,
never bothers us in the dining room; it is only in the Church that it causes
us to hesitate.

Memoirs, pp. 509-510.

Patience

The river also teaches a sublime lesson in patience. It has taken ages
for it to do its work, and in that work every drop of water has played its
part. It takes time for individuals or groups of individuals to accomplish
a great work and because time is required those who labor in behalf of their
fellows sometimes become discouraged. Nature teaches us to labor and to wait.
Viewed from day to day the progress of the race is imperceptible; viewed from
year to year, it can scarcely be noted, but viewed by decades or centuries the
upward trend is apparent, and every good work and word and thought contributes

toward the final result. As nothing is lost in the economy of nature, so nothing is lost in the social and moral world. As the stream is composed of an innumerable number of rivulets, each making its little offering and each necessary to make up the whole, so the innumerable number of men and women who recognize their duty to society and their obligations to their fellows are contributing according to their strength to the sum total of the forces that make for righteousness and progress.

Memoirs pp. 508-509.

Peace of Mind

Some have sought peace in social distinction, but whether they have been within the charmed circle and fearful lest they might fall out, or outside, and hopeful that they might get in, they have not found peace . . I am glad that our Heavenly Father did not make the peace of the human heart to depend upon our ability to buy it with money, secure it in society, or win it at the polls, for in either case but few could have obtained it, but when He made peace the reward of a conscience void of offense toward God and man, He put it within the reach of all. The poor can secure it as easily as the rich, the social outcasts as freely as the leader of society, and the humblest citizen equally with those who wield political power.

Speeches, Vol II, p. 281.

Child of Fortune

I have been the child of fortune from my birth. God gave me into the keeping of a Christian father and a Christian mother. They implanted in my heart the ideals that have guided my life.

Speeches, Vol II, pp. 416-417.

Truth in the Bible

I am not ashamed to quote from the Bible, for I have never found any other book which contains so much of truth, nor have I found any other book in which truth was so well expressed. You will remember that the disciples quarreled among themselves as to which should be the greatest in the kingdom of Heaven, and when they brought the question to the Master, he said: "Let him who would be chiefest among you be the servant of all." Service is the measure of greatness. It always has been true; it is true today; it always will be true that he is greatest who does the most good.

Under Other Flags, pp. 252-253.

If to the encouragement that my words may bring to the young men of our land I can add a moral, it is this: Truth, being of God, is omnipotent. It has within itself the power to propagate itself. Man can delay, but cannot prevent its triumph. Man borrows more strength from a great truth than he gives to it. It is of little importance to truth whether any individual espouses it, but to the individual it is of vital importance that he shall know the truth, and knowing it, adhere to it.

Jefferson said that he had learned that firm adherence to principle was the best handmaiden, even unto ambition.

If my Memoirs prove of benefit to others they will pay in part the debt I owe to those who in the past have contributed to the spread of the Christian religion, the safe-guarding of society, and the establishing of popular government - the causes to which the mature years of my life have been dedicated.

Memoirs, Preface, p. 13.

CHAPTER

III

MEMORIES OF YOUTH

Family Home

In the spring of 1866 my father decided to move to the country, the reason being that he thought a farm a better place to raise a family.

The house was of brick and faced to the east and had a porch set in on the front and back side of the main living room. A piano was the principal piece of furniture in the parlor and is often recalled. One of the pictures most clearly outlined in my memory is the picture of the family gathered in this room on Sunday afternoon, singing Sunday-school songs and church hymns. Mother played the accompaniment and led in the singing. The Bryan Choir, as father called it, joined with youthful enthusiasm. Father's favorite piece was "Kind Words" and we were wont to close the singing with his favorite song. To these Sunday afternoon exercises, as well as to the Sunday school, I am indebted for these tunes that have run through my mind ever since.

The spare bedroom was set apart for the special entertainment of politicians and divines. The bringing together of these two classes illustrated not only my father's views on the subjects but early taught me to regard the science of government as an entirely honorable one. My father was as much at home with ministers as he was with politicians and statesmen. He saw no necessary conflict - and I have never been able to see any - between the principles of our government and the principles of Christian faith.

Memoirs, pp. 32-34.

Value of Corporal Punishment

My parents believed in the old adage, "Spare the rod and spoil the child," and as they loved me too well to risk my being spoiled, they punished me. As I look back upon these punishments, I find myself more tolerant in passing judgment upon them than I was at the time, although I recall instances where I recognized the punishment as just, and some instances where I felt that I deserved more than I received. They were quite strict with me and I sometimes considered the boys more fortunate who were given more liberty, but on reflection I am not prepared to say that I would have done better under a different system. Other kinds of discipline may be better for other children - that parents must decide for themselves. I am not only satisfied but grateful for the punishment I received.

Memoirs, p. 40.

First Lessons

At the age of ten I was sent to school; before that time my mother taught me at home. Grandma's room - the back sitting room - was my first schoolhouse, and a little walnut table about two feet square, as my memory reproduces it to-day, was the first stump from which I made a speech. I would learn my lessons until I could repeat questions and answers without the book and then I would stand up on this little table and declaim them to my mother. My first audience, therefore, was a receptive, appreciative, and enthusiastic one.

Memoirs, p. 40.

Early Speaking

I began very young to manifest an interest in speaking and received all the encouragement that a child could from both father and mother. As the pro-fession which I liked leads up to forensics efforts, it must also be taken into consideration no child could have had an environment more favorable to a public career or stronger incentives to follow this particular line of work.

Memoirs, p. 41.

School Record

During these five years in the public school I do not recall much that is worth recording. I walked in to school, a distance of three-quarters of a mile to the first building and about a mile to the second and to the high school. I was regular in attendance and studious, having behind me the coercive power of parents who were determined that I should have an education. I do not recall that I ever failed in an examination, neither do I remember to have been at the head of the class in these earlier days. I might have been called an average - I was not below the average in my studies and well toward the front in deport-ment. In the high school I began studying Latin and also went a step forward in the art of declamation in the literary society work. We had a debating club in the high school and I recall taking a part in what we called The Senate, and I was a senator from Illinois. It may have been that this experience in a "senate" suggested to me the thought of being some time a Senator of the United States. This ambition received encouragement from my father's race for Congress in 1872 when I was twelve years old.

I early became interested in the political news in the papers and recall very distinctly the eagerness with which I searched the columns of the Missouri Republican, the first prominent political newspaper I ever read.

Memoirs, pp. 40-42.

Influence of Bible

My father, being a very devout man, lost no opportunity to impress upon me the value of the Bible. To him it was not only the Word of God but the fountain of Wisdom. He was especially fond of Proverbs and was in the habit of calling me in from work a little before noon to read a chapter and comment upon it. I cannot say that I shared his enthusiasm at the time - in fact, I was at times a little restless and even wished that I might have been allowed to devote the time to work in the field rather than to the reading and comments. But when he died, soon after I was twenty, the Biblical truths that he sought to impress upon me grew in value and I took up the book of Proverbs and read it through once a month for a year. I have frequently mentioned this experience and advised young men to read Proverbs because of the accumulated wisdom to be found therein - wisdom on all moral questions and expressed with wonderful force and clearness. I have quoted from Proverbs in my political speeches more than from any other part of the Bible or from any other book. Solomon left a rare collection of epigrams and it was the reading of Proverbs that gave me my first appreciation of the value of epigrams.

Memoirs, pp. 43-44.

Religious Training and Conversion

My religious training was not neglected at any period of my life. We had family prayers - one of the sweetest recollections of my boyhood days - and I entered Sunday school early. My father being a Baptist and my mother being a Methodist, I went to both Sunday schools. The only advantage that I know of that can come from the parents belonging to different churches is that the Sunday school opportunities are doubled. I would not offer this as sufficient reason for encouraging a difference in church membership on the part of parents, but where there is a difference of this kind, the Sunday school may, to some extent, be an off-setting advantage - at least, in my case it gave to me the double interest in Sunday-school work, an interest which has never waned.

At the age of fourteen I reached one of the turning points in my life. I attended a revival that was being conducted in a Presbyterian church and was converted. Having been brought up in a Christian home, conversion did not mean a change in my habits of life or habits of thought. I do not know of a virtue that came into my life as a result of my joining the Church, because all the virtues had been taught me by my parents. Truthfulness had been so earnestly enjoined that in more than one case I received my parents' commendation for not misrepresenting the situation when truthfulness might bring criticism if not punishment.

Memoirs, p. 44.

Reward for Truth

I remember that one day we children were playing in the sitting room, and noticing father's pocketbook upon the bureau, it occurred to some one of us - I do not know which - to count the money, so we locked the door and proceeded to inform ourselves upon the amount in the pocketbook. When we were just finishing we heard his footfall in the hall. We hurriedly crowded the money into the pocketbook and opened the door, but not soon enough to avoid suspicion. When he found me alone he asked me what we were doing. I told him we were count-

ing his money, whereupon he took me down town and bought me a saddle, presenting it and telling me, as he presented it, to remember I received it for telling the truth. I do not know of any similar amount of money that ever made so
great an impression upon my youthful mind and heart.

As an illustration of the teaching which I received at home I cite two
other instances. Before entering school at the age of ten my mother so impressed upon me her opinion of swearing - a matter in which my father also set me
a valuable example - that when I entered school I felt a distinct aversion to
swearing. I would find myself withdrawing from the crowd when the boys began
to swear, and to this day I have not overcome the aversion which I felt in
those early days.

Memoirs, pp. 44-45.

Parents Religious Flexibility

There is one fact in connection with my early days that should, I think,
be recorded, namely, my parents' willingness to allow me to choose at that early
age a church different from their own. It was an evidence of their liberality
in denominational matters, notwithstanding the deep and permanent convictions
which they had on Christian fundamentals. I noted this liberality first in the
attitude of each in the other's church before they became members of the same
church. I noticed it also in their treatment of ministers of the various
churches who were occasionally assembled at our house at family dinner. I was
also impressed by the fact that when we gathered our hay my father was in the
habit of sending a load away to each minister, including the Catholic priest
when a priest resided there.

This liberality was also proof of the deep concern about my religious life.
When I asked my father whether he had any objections to my joining the Presbyterian Church - my inclination to join being based upon two facts: first, my
conversion at a revival held in that Church; and second being the fact that
some seventy young people of the Sunday school, my schoolmates in the day school,
joined at that time - he said that he wanted me to join where I felt I would
be most at home and could do the most good. I never knew until after his death
that he was disappointed that I did not become a member of his own church.

Memoirs, pp. 48-49.

Importance of Religious Environment

As I look back over the years, I am increasingly grateful for the religious
environment that surrounded me in my youth and the devotion of my parents and
for the influence that the Church had upon me in my school days. The period
through which one passes in the journey from youth to maturity is quite likely
to be accompanied by some religious uncertainty. In the course of nature the
child will substitute the spirit of independence for the spirit of dependence.
Instead of doing things because he is told to, he must do them upon his own responsibility and from his own convictions. During this transition period the

pendulum is apt to swing too far and he sometimes finds himself more self-reliant than he ought to be and less disposed to be influenced by advice of others. It is just at this time when the parental authority is weakening that usually the student begins in the study of the physical sciences. If he is fortunate enough to have teachers who are themselves Christians with a spiritual vision of life, the effect is to strengthen his faith and he advances to a normal religious life. If he is unfortunate enough to fall under the influence of mind worshipers, he may be led step by step away from faith into unbelief. It is a matter of profound gratitude to me that during these days I was associated with Christian instructors so that the doubts aroused by my studies were resolved by putting them beside a powerful and loving God. Knowledge of the experiences of students has made me very sympathetic with students in college and has led me to go from college to college in the hope of helping young men to find solid ground upon which to stand. It was this interest in young men more than anything else which led me to prepare and deliver the address entitled, "The Prince of Peace."

Memoirs, pp. 50-51.

Financial Accounting

When I left home for school father told me that he was unable to furnish me with the money that I actually needed but that he could not afford to have me waste money; and then he suggested what I have always believed to be a good rule, that I should keep an account and report to him the use I had already made of the money when I wrote for more. This I proceeded to do and I do not recall that he ever referred to the expenditures except in one case.

Memoirs, p. 54.

Father's Advice

When I first left home I was growing very rapidly. I have reason to remember, because I wrote back home for money to buy a new pair of pants, explaining to my father that my pants had become so short that I was ashamed to attend the church sociables. He wrote back saying that I would soon be home for the holidays and could then replenish my wardrobe and added, "But you might as well learn now that people will measure you by the length of your head and not by the length of your breeches."

When I went home from college for a vacation we happened to weigh at the same time. He weighed 154 and I weighed 150. I was rather proud of my weight and said, "I shall soon be as heavy as you are." He replied with a twinkle of the eye, "When you have four pounds more of brains we will weigh the same." The next time we weighed I weighed more than he did and recalling his remark I attributed all the increase as "brain weight."

Memoirs, p. 56.

College Courses

I took the classical course, not as a matter of choice, because I had no choice in the matter. My father and mother decided that question and told me what I was to do, as they had decided for me the question of going to college. I do not know the date of the decision; I only know that from my earliest recollection I was going to college and was going to take the highest course. When I left home, father took from his library two of the largest books, a Greek lexicon and a Latin lexicon, and told me that I was to use the former for six years in the study of Greek and the latter five years in the study of Latin. I did not then know of their importance, but have since been very glad that there were others wiser than myself to decide such questions for me. I have come to place a high estimate upon the study of the dead languages because of the training they give one in the choice of words and because of the acquaintance that they give the student with the derivation of words. I liked Latin better than the Greek - possibly because it is easier. I became so attached to the Latin that I planned to read some Latin every year as a recreation. But I soon became occupied with work which was necessary so the sentimental was crowded out.

Mathematics was my favorite study until I took up political economy. During the senior year of my preparatory work I took freshman college mathematics and was marked one hundred in geometry. I was a contestant for the freshman prize in mathematics with Sam Montgomery, a boy who was taking the scientific course. I do not know which had the highest marks, because I learned before the prize was awarded that the competition was open only to those who were in the freshman class.

Memoirs, pp. 58-59.

Prizes for Education

I felt the lure of prizes from the start and took part in every contest for which I was eligible. A prize stirred me to activity, and a recollection of its influence upon my studies has led me in later days to stimulate students to similar activity by the establishing of prizes in a number of institutions of learning.

Memoirs, p. 85.

CHAPTER

IV

PUBLIC SPEAKING

"In no quality did Bryan shine more conspicuously or appear more effective than in his ability, by his oratory, to lift men to a higher plane of idealism. He could make the commonest, dullest man see the superior qualities in other men and in broad human issues. He thought constantly in terms of human welfare and no matter how abstruse the question, or how technical the material or issues, Bryan's fine emotional nature and his great idealism caused him to present those issues not as mere matters of dollars and cents, but as great questions of human rights, human advancement and human welfare. He could take a crowd of men who had been feeling blue, and lift them to a high plane of spiritual exaltation, sending them out charged with his own dynamic personality and his high idealism."

Williams, p. 503.

Declamation Contest

In my first year in the academy - "Junior Prep" as it was called - I entered the declamation contest, using as my theme Patrick Henry's famous speech, "Give me liberty or give me death." The judges did not seem to regard me as especially promising. At any rate, I was not near enough to even second place to give me any intense interest in the returns. The next year I entered the declamation contest again, this time taking as my subject by the advice of Mrs. Jones, "The Palmetto and the Pine." The sentiment was most excellent, but my delivery seemed to lack something - enough to enable two of the contestants to pass me. I came third in the estimate of the judges and Dr. Jones thought that my failure may have been due to indistinctness of articulation. I do not know whether that was true or not, but it spurred me up on that particular subject and distinctness of articulation became a controlling passion with me.

In the freshman year I entered the declamation contest for the third time, after having divided the second prize in Latin prose composition with a fellow student. I was gaining ground. In my first contest I came down toward the last, in my second contest I ranked third, in my third contest I won half of the second prize, in my fourth contest - I rose a point higher and had the second prize all to myself.

Memoirs, pp. 85-86.

Public Speaking Training

I digress here to say that I received the usual training in public speaking. Professor Hamilton was our instructor; he was a large man with a strong face and a piercing eye. He rather leaned to the dramatic and recommended dramatic pieces to us. I rather preferred the oratorical style. He complimented me by saying that I declaimed the oratorical pieces so well that he could not be of much assistance to me along that line. He trained us in modulation of the voice, gesticulation, etc., and I presume that his instructions were beneficial to me, although I have been so much more interested in the subject matter than in the form of presentation that my use of his advice has been unconscious rather than intentional.

As our absorption of ideals is gradual and constant, I do not know to what extent I am indebted to him for the settled opinions which I have formed on public speaking. I think that the instruction in gesticulation becomes valuable as one forgets the instructions and moves his arms and body without thought of the instructions. It is hard to be graceful in gesticulation when one is thinking about the movements to be made, just as it is difficult for one to speak naturally while he is engaged in artificial effort. But the training that one receives, both in the modulation of the voice and in action, finally becomes a part of him - a second nature, so to speak - and he obeys the suggestions that he has received without a thought.

In my sophomore year I entered the contest in essay and won the first prize - with an essay on the by no means novel subject of "Labor." This pleased my father more than the previous prizes won. He said that he would rather have me gain prominence for my own thoughts than by repeating the words of others.

Memoirs, p. 87.

Advice from Gen. John C. Black

In the following October (1880) I went to Galesburg, Illinois, to represent my college in the contest to which I had looked forward for many years. My subject was "Justice." After the prize had been awarded, General John C. Black of Chicago, with whom I afterwards served in Congress, one of the judges in this contest, took me to his room in the hotel and gave me encouragement and advice. He told me that he had marked me one hundred on delivery and high enough on thought and composition to make me his first choice (the marks of the other two brought me down to second place). He then gave me his advice on various styles of oratory, contrasting the style of Edmund Burke, whose sentences were long and involved, and the style of Victor Hugo, whose sentences were short and pithy. He said that I leaned rather to the style of the latter and advised me to cultivate longer sentences. I have not forgotten his advice, but have found it difficult to follow it, possibly because I have always labored under the coercion that made me so anxious to present a subject clearly that I could not give much attention to ornamentation and figures of speech.

Memoirs, p. 89.

Speech Introduction

In my oration on "Justice" my introduction was, I think, as appropriate as any that I have ever employed. I learned quite early the wisdom of a beginning that immediately catches the attention. I noticed this in speeches, of which I early became an eager reader, and observed Wendell Phillips when he delivered his famous lecture, "The Lost Arts," at Jacksonville during my student days.

Memoirs, p. 89.

Prize Money

My speech on Justice began: "Plutarch tells us that men entertain three sentiments concerning the gods; they fear them for their power, respect them for their intelligence, and love them for their justice." The local paper had a complimentary account of my speech - they generally praised where they could performance of students - and these early bits of eulogy are very satisfying to participants in contests - especially those who fail to win prizes. I came second, my college backer insisting, as college boys are wont to do, that I ought to have had first place.

The fifty dollars handed me by the treasurer of the oratorical association was the largest sum that I had earned up to that time. The first draft upon me was made for the purchase of an engagement ring for my intended wife. I had waited from June until October in order to purchase the ring with money that I had myself earned. It was a modest ring - a garnet set in gold - but it was sufficient to satisfy our simple tastes, and adorn Mrs. Bryan's hand until it was lost during the campaign of 1896. It was my custom to earn the money to pay for any gifts to Miss Baird, and during a large part of my college days I added to my spending money by clerking in a hat store on Saturdays.

Memoirs, p. 91.

Essence of Moulding Public Opinion

The moulding of public opinion is one of the greatest of the arts, and the essence of moulding public opinion lies in the ability to say much in a few words. No uninspired writer has left so much of wisdom contained in so small a compass. One of the proverbs of Solomon which I early learned and often quoted was "A prudent man forseeth the evil, and hideth himself." This cannot be improved upon so far as the sentiment is concerned or the beauty of expression, but I found that audiences - especially students - did not seem to grasp it. As the object of speaking is to impress truth, I finally took the liberty of presenting this truth in a way most familiar to the student and most easily remembered. The paraphrase ran like this, "The prudent man gets the idea into his head, the foolish man gets it in the neck." The students instantly caught the idea and I felt that the impressing of the idea did more good than the slang did harm. The consolation of the reformer is that if he is right in uttering the warning and the people do not heed, they will come to him when their necks are sore.

Memoirs, p. 43.

Speak to the Heart

I do not address myself primarily to your heads, for it is a poor head that can not find a reason for doing what the heart wants to do. I desire rather to speak to your hearts. The Bible says: "As a man thinketh in his heart, so he is." I want you to ask yourselves whether there is any other measure of your responsibility and mine than the measure which we find in Holy Writ - a measure which makes us not only serve, but serve to the extent that we have power and opportunity.

Commoner, Vol V, p. 436.

Theme More Important than Speaker

While I appreciate kindly feeling and expressions of confidence and respect, I am very much more anxious that I shall impress my theme upon you tonight, than that I shall impress myself - in fact, I am comparatively indifferent as to what you may think of me, if I can make you think of the subject to which I invite your attention.

Commoner, p. 427.

Essentials of Public Speaking

Webster, the great orator, said of eloquence that it must exist "in the man, in the subject, and in the occasion." And then he proceeded to elaborate the statement, showing that it was a combination of high purpose, firm resolve, and dauntless spirit, speaking from every feature and reaching the heart of the hearer. There are two things absolutely essential to eloquence. First, the speaker must know what he is talking about, and, second, he must mean what he says. Nothing can take the place of knowledge of the subject and earnestness. To these other things can be added, such as clearness of statement, felicity of expression, aptness in illustration, beauty in ornamentation and grace in delivery.

Eloquence is heart speaking to heart. There is no mistaking the cry of terror or the shout of joy, and so there is no misunderstanding the sincere message that passes from heart to heart.

The young man who would fit himself for real influence in the forum must himself feel deeply upon the subjects which he discusses, and he cannot feel deeply without being in full-sympathy with those whom he addresses. He must also be able to give them information which they do not possess or to state what they know more forcibly than they can state it themselves....

A knowledge of human nature is necessary to the orator. Pope has said that the proper study of mankind is man, and in the study of man the heart is the most interesting as well as the most important subject of investigation. He who would succeed in public speaking must understand that a sense of justice is the safest foundation upon which to build a government. Bancroft, in the address above referred to, declares that popular government is the strongest government in the world, because "discarding the implements of terror, it dares to rule by moral force and has its citadel in the heart."

Moral courage is indispensable to the orator. A man cannot speak eloquently while he is running from the enemy; neither can he inspire courage if his knees smite each other, and there is a tremor in his voice. Courage rests upon conviction; a man has no convictions to speak of, who is not willing to endure suffering in support of them.

The orator must have faith - faith in God, faith in the righteousness of his cause, and faith in the ultimate triumph of the truth. Believing that right makes might, believing that every word spoken for truth and every act done in behalf of truth contributes to the final victory, he does his duty, more anxious to help the cause which he espouses than to enjoy the fruits of victory.

And, finally, let the ambitious young man understand that he is in duty bound to discard everything which in the least weakens his strength, and under obligation to do everything that in any degree increases his power to do good. Good habits, therefore, are always important, and may become vitally so.

Memoirs, pp. 258-261.

CHAPTER

V

RELIGIOUS BELIEFS

Study of Creation

It was at this period that I became confused by the different theories of creation. But I examined these theories and found that they all assumed something to begin with. You can test this for yourselves. The nebular hypothesis, for instance, assumes that matter and force existed - matter in particles infinitely fine and each particle separated from every other particle by space infinitely great. Beginning with this assumption, force working on matter - according to this hypothesis - created a universe. Well, I have a right to assume, and I prefer to assume, a Designer back of the design - a Creator back of the creation; and no matter how long you draw out the process of creation, so long as God stands back of it you cannot shake my faith in Jehovah. In Genesis it is written that, in the beginning, God created the heavens and the earth, and I can stand on that proposition until I find some theory of creation that goes farther back than "the beginning:. We must begin with something - we must start somewhere - and the Christian begins with God.

Speeches, Vol II, p. 266.

Belief in God

I believe in God; I believe that He influences the thoughts and the purposes of men; but I am not willing to blame God for every thought and every purpose that a man may have. If I feel in my heart an impulse to do wrong, I will not blame Him. If I feel in my heart an impulse to do good, I will trace it to God. If I feel in my heart an impulse to put my hand into my own pocket and take my money and give it to some one in distress I will trace the impulse to God; but if I feel in my heart an impulse to put my hand into some other person's pocket and take his money, I will not lay it onto the Almighty; there is another old fellow that I will lay it on.

Life and Speeches, p. 81.
Speech in Baltimore, January 20, 1900.

Creator in Silence

The investigation of science ought to increase rather than diminish reverence for the Creator, for each new discovery proves more clearly the wisdom and power of the great Designer. The patterns that He has set invite limitless effort. The soap bubble presents a combination of colors that the artist has thus far failed to match; a pint of water holds a latent energy which no giant can boast; the trembling leaf contains a laboratory more complete than the chemist has been able to construct; the tiniest seed that falls to the ground possesses a potency that man has not yet fathomed. Working in the midst of mysteries and dumb in the presence of daily miracle of life we are constantly gathering evidence of the loving kindness of the Infinite Intelligence who has so bountifully provided for the supplying of every human need.

Commoner, Vol V, p. 331.

Miracles

I will not deny that God does perform a miracle or may perform one merely because I do not know how or why He does it. I find it so difficult to decide each day what God wants done now that I am not presumptuous enough to attempt to declare what God might have wanted to do thousands of years ago. The fact that we are constantly learning of the existence of new forces suggests the possibility that God may operate through forces yet unknown to us, and the mysteries with which we deal every day warn me that faith is as necessary as sight. Who would have credited a century ago the stories that are now told of the wonder-working electricity? For ages man had known the lightning, but only to fear it; now, this invisible current is generated by a man-made machine, imprisoned in a man-made wire and made to do the bidding of man. We are even able to dispense with the wire and hurl words through space, and the x-ray has enabled us to look through substances which were supposed, until recently, to exclude all light. The miracle is not more mysterious than many of the things with which man now deals - it is simply different.

Speeches, Vol II, p. 270.

Origin of Life

It is true that man, in some physical characteristics resembles the beast, but man has a mind as well as a body, and a soul as well as a mind. The mind is greater than the body and the soul is greater than the mind, and I object to having man's pedigree traced on one-third of him only - and that the lowest third. The ape, according to this theory, is older than man and yet the ape is still an ape while man is the author of the marvelous civilization which we see about us.

One does not escape from mystery, however, by accepting this theory, for it does not explain the origin of life. When the follower of Darwin has traced the germ of life back to the lowest form in which it appears - and to follow him one must exercise more faith than religion calls for - he finds that scientists differ. Those who reject the idea of creation are divided into two schools, some believing that the first germ of life came from another planet and others holding that it was the result of spontaneous generation. Each school answers the arguments advanced by the other, and as they cannot agree with each other, I am not compelled to agree with either.

If I were compelled to accept one of these theories I would prefer the first, for if we can chase the germ of life off this planet and get it out into space we can guess the rest of the way and no one can contradict us, but if we accept the doctrine of spontaneous generation we cannot explain why spontaneous generation ceased to act after the first germ was created.

Go back as far as we may, we cannot escape from the creative act, and it is just as easy for me to believe that God created man <u>as he is</u> as to believe that, millions of years ago, He created a germ of life and endowed it with power to develop into all that we see today. I object to the Darwinian theory, until more conclusive proof is produced, because I fear we shall lose the consciousness of God's presence in our daily life, if we must accept the theory that through all the ages no spiritual force has touched the life of man or shaped the destiny of nations.

Speeches, Vol II, pp. 267-268.

Scopes Trial

My Dear Mr. - - :

I am not able to terminate our long friendship as cheerfully as you do, and I shall not allow a difference of opinion on religion to blot out the pleasant memory of earlier days.

I am glad, however, that something deters you from appearing in the Tennessee case - I only wish it were something less serious than advancing years. Among the people of Colorado who have honored you in the past, there are many who believe in revealed religion and who would be as much distressed at your appearance on the side of those who attack revealed religion as you are at my connection with the other side of the case, still respecting you, they could not feel as bitterly toward you as you do toward me. I have passed through so many controversies that caused realignment among friends that I have become accustomed to both losses and accretions. In this controversary, I have a larger majority on my side than in any previous controversary, and I have more intolerant opponents that I ever had in politics.

Memoirs, pp. 303-304.

Faith Necessary to Accept Materialism

I have been reading a book recently on materialism and I have been interested in the attempt of the author to drive God out of the universe. He searches for Him with a microscope, and He is too small to see; then he searches for Him with a telescope, and because he cannot see Him among the stars or beyond, he declares that there is no God - that matter and force alone are eternal, and that force acting on matter has produced the clod, the grass that grows upon the clod, the beast that feeds upon the grass, and man, the climax of created things. I have tried to follow his reasoning and have made up my mind that it requires more faith to accept the scientific demonstrations of materialism than to accept any religion I have ever known.

Speeches, Vol II, p. 244.

God in a Watermelon

I was eating a piece of watermelon some months ago and was struck with its beauty. I took some of the seeds and dried them and weighed them, and found that it would require some five thousand seeds to weigh a pound; and then I applied mathematics to that forty-pound melon. One of these seeds, put into the ground, when warmed by the sun and moistened by the rain, takes off its coat and goes to work; it gathers from somewhere two hundred thousand times its own weight, and forcing this raw material through a tiny stem, constructs a watermelon. It ornaments the outside with a covering of green; inside the green it puts a layer of white, and within the white a core of red, and all through the red it scatters seeds, each one capable of continuing the work of reproduction. Who drew the plan by which that little seed works? Where does it get its tremendous strength? Where does it find its coloring matter? How does it collect its flavoring extract? How does it develop a watermelon? Until you can explain a watermelon, do not be too sure that you can set limits to the power of the Almighty and say just what He would do or how He would do it.

Speeches, Vol II, p. 272.

Immortality

If the Father deigns to touch with divine power the cold and pulseless heart of the buried acorn and to make it burst forth from its prison walls, will He leave neglected in the earth the soul of man, made in the image of his Creator? If He stoops to give to the rose bush, whose withered blossoms float upon the autumn breeze, the sweet assurance of another springtime, will He refuse the words of hope to the sons of men when the frosts of winter come? If matter, mute and inanimate, though changed by the forces of nature into a multitude of forms, can never die, will the imperial spirit of man suffer annihilation when it has paid a brief visit like a royal guest to this tenement of clay? No, I am sure that He who, notwithstanding His apparent prodigality, created nothing without a purpose, and wasted not a single atom in all His creation, has made provision for a future life in which man's universal longing for immortality will find its realization. I am as sure that we live again as I am that we live today.

Memoirs, p. 510

Resurrection

In Cairo I secured a few grains of wheat that had slumbered for more than thirty centuries in an Egyptian tomb. As I looked at them this thought came into my mind: If one of those grains had been planted on the banks of the Nile the year after it grew, and all its lineal descendants had been planted and replanted from that time until now, its progeny would today be sufficiently numerous to feed the teeming millions of the world. An unbroken chain of life connects the earliest grains of wheat with the grains that we sow and reap. There is in the grain of wheat an invisible something which has the power to discard the body that we see, and from earth and air fashion a new body so like the old one that we cannot tell the one from the other. If this invisible germ of life in the grain of wheat can thus pass unimpaired through three thousand resurrections, I shall not doubt that my soul has power to clothe itself with a body suited to its new existence when this earthly frame has crumbled into dust.

Memoirs, p. 511.

Religious Tolerance

My attitude on the subject of religious tolerance has been inherited, so to speak, from my parents. In memory of these religious social gatherings my good wife has been led to set aside certain days for the bringing together of the representatives of the various denominations in a social way.

Memoirs, p. 28.

Association with Many Religions

I have not put great emphasis upon church lines, or church doctrines, for I am connected by ties of blood with several churches, and by ties of friendship with all the other churches. I find that I am recalling more and more frequently a story which I heard when I was a boy; it has really had a great deal of influence in shaping my views on church questions. It was in a southern Methodist church that I heard it. The minister said that there was a mill and that many people brought wheat to the mill by several roads. When they arrived with the wheat - some coming by one road and some by another - some over the hill and some along the stream - the miller never asked them by what road they came, but simply whether the wheat was good.

Commoner, Vol V, p. 426.

God and the Election

Two colored preachers down in Georgia were discussing religion, as they are wont to do sometimes, and the Presbyterian brother was trying to persuade the Methodist, and the Methodist brother hung back on the doctrine of election. The Presbyterian brother said: "Its just this way - the voting is going on all the time; the Lord is voting for you and the devil is voting against you, and whichever way you vote, that's the way the election goes.

Commoner, Vol V, pp. 426-427.

Love over War

But overshadowing all other Napoleonic monuments is his home on the banks
of the Seine, adjoining the Invalides. Its gilded dome attracts attention
from afar, and on nearer approach one is charmed with the strength of its walls
and the symetry of its proportions.

At the door the guard cautions the thoughtless to enter with uncovered
head, but the admonition is seldom necessary, for an air of solemnity pervades
the place.

In the center of the rotunda, beneath the frescoed vault of the great dome,
is a circular crypt. Leaning over the heavy marble balustrade I gazed on the
massive sarcophagus below which contains all that was mortal of that marvelous
combination of intellect and will.

The sarcophagus is made of dark red porphyry, a fitly chosen stone that
might have been colored by the mingling of the intoxicating wine of ambition
with the blood spilled to satisfy it.

Looking down upon the sarcophagus and the stands of tattered battle flags
that surround it, I reviewed the tragic career of this grand master of the art
of slaughter, and weighed, as best I could, the claims made for him by his
friends. And then I found myself wondering what the harvest might have been
had Napoleion's genius led him along the peaceful paths, had the soil of Europe
been stirred by the plowshare rather than by his trenchant blade, and the
reaping done by implements less destructive than his shot and shell.

Just beyond and above the entombed emperor stands a cross upon which hangs
a life-size figure of the Christ, flooded by a mellow lemon-colored light, which
pours through the stained glass windows of the chapel.

Whether so intended or not, it will, to those who accept the teachings of
the Sermon on the Mount, symbolize love's final victory over force and the
triumph of that philosophy which finds happiness in helpful service and glory
in doing good.

Old World, p. 520.

Death God's Way

To the young, death is an appalling thing, but it ought not to be to those
whose advancing years warn them of its certain approach. As we journey along
life's road we must pause again and again to bid farewell to some fellow
traveler. In the course of nature the father and mother die, then brothers and
sisters follow, and finally the children and the children's children cross to
the unknown world beyond - one by one "from love's shining circle the gems drop
away" until the "king of terrors" loses his power to affright us and the increasing company on the farther shore makes us first willing and then anxious
to join them. It is God's way. It is God's way.

Under Other Flags, p. 382.

Opposing Forces of Government

There are two forces constantly at work in every nation, one force tending to bring the government nearer to the people and the other tending to carry the government away from the people. To go a little farther back we may start with the proposition that there are but two theories of government - one that a government is a thing created by the people for themselves - this is the theory which is embodied in our Declaration of Independence, which declares that governments derive their just powers from the consent of the governed. The opposite theory is that governments are imposed by the few upon the many - such governments resting on force. Few, if any governments now known entirely exemplify either theory - nearly all, if not all, of them representing a compromise between the two theories, but in every government there is a tendency either in one direction or the other.

Commoner, Vol V, pp. 273-274

Rights of Man

The declaration that all men are created equal means that men are created equal in their natural rights. It means that God never gave to one human being a single natural right that he did not give to every other human being, and among these rights the Declaration of Independence enumerates the right to live, the right to liberty and the right to the pursuit of happiness.

Under Other Flags, p. 266.

Strength of Democracy

The old saying, that "everybody knows more than anybody", is founded upon reason and experience, but there is another reason why a democracy is better than an aristocracy, namely, that the interests of the whole people are safer in the hands of the people themselves than in the hands of any element which assumes to speak for the people. The faults of free government have been found to be, not in the people themselves, but in those who, selected to represent them, betray their trust. If the representatives of the people whom the people themselves select are sometimes unfaithful to their trust, what must be expected of those who assume to act without being selected by the people?

Old World, p. 489.

CHAPTER

VI

DEFINITION OF DEMOCRACY

Rule of Majority

There is no reason to believe that a majority or a minority will always be right. There is, however, reason to believe that the rule of the majority is more apt to be right than the rule of a minority. Truth has in it such a persuasive power that a minority in possession of truth generally grows into a majority, but until it becomes a majority it cannot insist upon recognition. If a majority makes mistakes, it must be remembered that a minority makes mistakes, too. And if the rule of the minority is substituted for the rule of the majority, there may be any number of minorities warring with each other for the right to speak for the whole. If we deny to the majority the right to rule, there is no basis upon which to build. If a minority rules it must rule by force, for the moment it secures the consent of the majority it is no longer a minority.

Commoner, Vol II, p. 25.

Democracy Founded on Brotherhood of Man

That democratic principles are sound does not, among democrats at least, admit of dispute for they rest upon the belief in the brotherhood of man. That those principles will triumph can not be doubted by those who believe in their truth, for truth is mighty, and must at last prevail.

If any of you lack faith, go forth into the fields, You find that a tiny seed planted in the ground contains a germ that, bursting from its prison walls, sends its roots down into the ground and its leaves up into the air. Under the influence of soil, and rain, and sunshine, that seed multiplies until it furnishes bread for the race. Go forth among the orchards and you will find that a little slip or twig will grow into a tree which will furnish shade for the weary, and fruit for the hungry. You know that behind the seed and the twig is an irresistible force that, working constantly, supplied the need of man. The force behind moral and economic fruit are not less irresistible. We have but to plant and attend them, and the harvest of blessing is sure.

Commoner, Vol V, p. 8.

Democracy is the Common People

But I want to speak of democracy in even a larger way, and that is as the term describes - the people at work - the common people, if you will. And when I say "the common people" let no one think that I use the term as a term of reproach.

Commoner, Vol V, p. 428.

Praise for Common People

The common people form the industrious, intelligent and patriotic element of our population; they produce the nation's wealth in times of peace and fight the nation's battles in time of war. They are self-reliant and independent; they ask of government nothing but justice and will not be satisfied with less. They are not seeking to get their hands into other people's pockets, but are content if they can keep other people's hands out of their pockets.

The commoner will be satisfied if, by fidelity to the common people, it proves its right to the name which has been chosen.

Commoner, Vol I, p. 1.

Highest Title Common Man

The highest compliment ever paid to any class of people was paid to those who are called the common people. When we use that term there are some who say that we are appealing to the passions of the masses; there are some who apply the name demagogue to anybody who speaks of the common people. When the meek and lowly Nazarene came to preach "peace on earth, good will toward men," He was not welcomed by those who "devour widow's houses and for a pretense make long prayers". By whom was He welcomed? The Scriptures tell us that when He gave that great commandment, "Thou shalt love thy neighbor as thyself". the common people heard him gladly. This, I repeat, is the highest compliment that has ever been paid to any class of people, and the common people are the only people who have ever received gladly the doctrines of humility and equality.

I do not mean to say that there have been no exceptions to the general rule. There have always been found among the richer classes those who were filled with the spirit of philanthropy, those who were willing to spend their lives in the uplifting of their fellows. But I am now speaking of general rules, not of exceptions. . . . Yet in spite of all these exceptions, the common people have been the great and controlling force which has lifted civilization to higher ground.

Life and Speeches, p. 311.

Every Citizen Important

Every citizen is a factor in our civilization, and by his conduct raises or lowers the level of that civilization. He cannot expect his neighbor to be more conscientious than himself; he cannot rely upon someone performing the duty that he ought himself to discharge. He owes it to his country, as well as to his generation and to posterity, to throw the weight of his influence upon the right side of every public question. For the proper discharge of his duties, he will require the highest form of moral courage.

Commoner, Vol VI, p. 1.

Democracy Perpetual

When the people are recognized as the source of power the government is perpetual because the people endure forever. The government then responds to their desires and conforms to their character; it can be made as good as they deserve to have and they are satisfied with it because it is their own handiwork. If it has evils those evils are endured because the people recognize that they themselves are to blame and that it is within their power to apply any needed remedy.

All history sustains the self-evident truths which form the foundation of the government deriving its just powers from the consent of the government. All history condemns a political structure which appeals only to fear and relies upon bayonets for its support.

Commoner, Vol I, p. 3.

Democracy and Aristocracy

Every well informed student of history will recognize this distinction. In every community you can draw a line separating the aristocrat from the democrat. It will not be a perpendicular line, nor will it be a horizontal line; it will not separate those of illustrious lineage from those of humble birth; it will not separate the rich from the poor; it will not separate the education from the uneducated; it will not be along lines of vocation or occupation; but it will separate those "with the tastes, spirit, assumption and traditions of the aristocracy" from those who "believe in a government controlled by the people and favor political and legal equality".

Commoner, Vol II, p. 249.

The Unfinished Form of Government

Each locality has its questions of interest; each state has subjects which arouse discussion; each nation has its issues of paramount importance, and the world has its problems. There are transient questions which come and go and questions which, like Tennyson's brook "go on forever". Each generation, in each country, meets the issues presented by conditions, but all the nations of the earth are constantly grappling with problems universal in their scope and everlasting in duration. In his famous oration at Gettysburg, Abraham Lincoln spoke of an "unfinished work" which those buried there had promoted and to which the living should dedicate themselves. Every generation finds an unfinished work when it enters upon life's stage and leaves the work unfinished when it departs. The work of civilization is ever an unfinished one for the reason that new problems present themselves as soon as present ones have been solved. In our trip around the world we have had an opportunity to note some of the problems which most concern all peoples at all times. The first concerns the legitimate sphere of government - what should the government, acting for all the people do, and what should be left of the individual? This problem is under consideration in every civilized nation, and no two nations have reached the same solution. At the two extremes stand the individualist and the socialist - the former jealously guarding the individual and opposing any encroachments upon his sphere of action, the latter emphasizing the work of the state and seeking to convert the work of production and the work of distribution into state functions. Between these extremes stand the mass of the people, governed more by the exigencies of each individual case than by the theories put forward by individualist and socialist. In some directions the governments of Europe and Asia have extended the sphere of the state beyond anything known in the United States; beyond anything attempted in the old world, but everywhere the tendency is to extend rather than to diminish the sphere of the state's activities.

Old World, p. 478.

Democracy Conducive to Highest Civilization

Our institutions rest upon the proposition that all men, being created equal, are entitled to equal consideration at the hands of the Government. Because all men are created equal, it follows that no citizen has a natural right to injure any other citizen. The main purpose of government being to protect all citizens in the enjoyment of life, liberty and the pursuit of happiness, this purpose must lead the Government, first, to avoid acts of affirmative injustice, and , second, to restrain each citizen from trespassing upon the rights of any other citizen.

A democratic form of government is conducive to the highest civilization because it opens before each individual the greatest opportunities for development, and stimulates to the highest endeavor by insuring to each the full enjoyment of all the rewards of toil except such contribution as is necessary to support the government which protects him. Democracy is indifferent to pedigree - it deals with the individual rather than with his ancestors. Democracy ignores differences in wealth - neither riches nor poverty can be invoked in behalf of or against any citizen. Democracy knows no creed; recognizing the right of each individual to worship God according to the dictates of his own conscience, it welcomes all to a common brotherhood and guarantees equal treatment to all, no matter in what church or through what forms they commune with their Creator.

Life and Speeches, pp. 356-357.

Common People Strength of Country

Lincoln said that God must have loved the common people because He made so many of them. The common people are very numerous, and the uncommon people are not nearly so important as they sometimes think they are. The common people of a nation are its strength; they produce the nation's wealth in time of peace; they are the ones who stand ready to sacrifice themselves for their country in

time of war. The common people furnish the students for your colleges. From
the ranks of the common people, too, all the occupations and professions of
the city are recruited.

Commoner, Vol V, p. 428.

Cultured Oppose Common People

If there are in this country today those who doubt the capacity of the
people for self-government, you do not find them among the common people -
you find them among the cultured. If there are those who are not willing
that the people shall govern themselves you will find them not among the
masses - but among the cultured. Jackson, when he thundered forth the same
doctrine, was not popular among the cultured. Even Lincoln, when he dared to
say that he did not have a political principle that he had not drawn from the
Declaration of Independence, was not popular among the cultured. Those who
have been pleading the cause of the people have not received as kindly hearing
among the cultured as they have among the poor. Why is it? It ought not to be.

Commoner, Vol V, p. 432.

Self-Evident Truths

When it is said that the truths set forth in the Declaration of Independence are self-evident truths, it simply means that they appeal to those who
are anxious to find the truth, and will be supported by those who have no
personal reason for rejecting the truth.

Commoner, Vol II, p. 96

Jefferson Cultured and Common Man

I commend Jefferson to the educated men of today. His culture connected
him with the educated and the refined, and yet his creed and principles made
him the comrade and work-fellow of the people. I am praying today that in our
college communities we may raise up an increasing number of men who can be
cultured without being weaned away from their sympathy with the common people.
Why was Jefferson a comrade with the people? Because he recognized that all
were made in the image of the same God whose likeness he bore; because he
wanted nothing for himself that he was not willing that they should also have.

Commoner, Vol V, p. 431.

Jefferson Confident of Triumph of Truth

Jefferson paid a tribute to the power of truth when he said that truth was able to overcome error in the open field; and it was this sublime confidence in the triumph of truth that distinguished him from many of the other great men of his time. In fact, of all the men who have lived upon this earth I know of no man who surpassed Jefferson in confidence in the ultimate triumph of truth; and, my friends, upon what can people build if not upon faith in truth? Take from man his belief in the triumph of that which is right and he builds upon the sand. Give a man an abiding faith in the triumph of that which is true, and you give him the foundation of a moral character that can withstand all temptation.

Commoner, Vol III, p. 102.

Jefferson for Religion of Love

He wanted our religion to rest on the basis of love and not on the basis of force; and, my friends, when we get down to the root of our government, and the root of our religion, we find that they alike rest on the doctrine of human brotherhood--"that all men are created equal". "That they are endowed by their Creator with certain inalienable rights", rights that government did not give, rights that government cannot take away, that the object of government is to secure to the individual the enjoyment of his inalienable rights and that governments derive "their just powers from the consent of the governed". But all of these things rest upon that conception of human brotherhood which one cannot have unless he has the love that is back of every great thought.

Commoner, Vol III, p. 104.

Jefferson Great Dreamer

No, I cannot claim a place among the dreamers, but there has been a great dreamer in the realm of statesmanship - Thomas Jefferson. He saw a people bowed beneath oppression and he had a vision of a self-governing nation, in which every citizen would be a sovereign. He put his visions upon paper, and for more than a century multitudes have been building. They are building at this temple in every nation; some day it will be completed and then the people of all the world will find protection beneath its roof and security within its walls. I shall be content if, when my days are numbered, it can be truthfully said of me that with such ability as I possess, and whenever opportunity offered, I labored faithfully with the multitude to build this building higher in my time.

Speeches, Vol II, p. 428.

Average Man Can Answer Moral Questions

It is not true that the laboring man is incompetent to decide the questions that concern him and his country. The great questions of politics involve moral questions, and questions of right and wrong can be decided by a laboring man as well as by anyone else. It is a common error to assume that the average man on the farm and in the workshop is not competent to deal with the problems of government. Jefferson pointed out this error and asserted that the principles of right and wrong were so easily discerned as not to require the aid of many councilors.

Commoner, Vol VI, p. 325.

Heroes of Peace

I am glad that this association is going to erect a monument to his memory. I say going to erect it, because I can not believe that the American people need more than an opportunity to contribute to insure their contribution. I want this monument to be in keeping with the services of the man. I want it to stand as high as the monuments erected to warriors; I want it to testify to the world that the heroes of peace are as great at the heroes of war; that those who save human life are as great as those who take it, even though they take it in defense of a righeous cause. I want this monument to testify that a man can live for his country as well as die for his country.

Commoner, Vol III, p. 105.
Speech of April 13, 1903, for Thomas Jefferson Association.

Land of Liberty

The main purpose of the founders of our government was to secure for themselves and for posterity the blessings of liberty, and that purpose has been faithfully followed up to this time. Our statesmen have opposed each other upon economic questions, but they have agreed in defending self-government as the controlling national idea.

On each returning 4th of July our people have met to celebrate the signing of the Declaration of Independence; their hearts have renewed their vows to free institutions and their voices have praised the forefathers whose wisdom, courage and patriotism made it possible for each succeeding generation to repeat the words: "My country, tis of thee, sweet land of liberty, of thee I sing".

Speeches, Vol II, p. 13.

Demagogue or Statesman

The difference between a demagogue and a statesman is that the former advocates what he thinks will be popular, regardless of the effect that it may ultimately have upon the people to whom he appeals; the statesman advocates what he believes to be the best for the country regardless of the immediate effect which it may have upon himself. One is willing to sacrifice the permanent interests of others to advance his own temporary interests, while the other is willing to sacrifice his own temporary interests to advance the public welfare. While the conduct of the statesman may seem unselfish, and is unselfish in the usual acceptation of that term, yet it is really an enlightened selfishness, for no man, when he takes a broad view of his own interests, can afford to accept an advantage which comes to him at the expense of his country. The statesman is building upon a firmer foundation than the demagogue, and in the end will find a more substantial reward for his self-denial than the demagogue will be able to secure for himself.

Memoirs, p. 260.

Discontent Precedes Reform

The reformer is generally accused of stirring up discontent. I desire to remind you that discontent lies at the foundation of all progress. So long as you are satisfied you never move forward. It is only when you are dissatisfied with present conditions that you try to improve them. Why, my friends, had our forefathers been satisfied with English political supremacy we never would have had a Declaration of Independence. They were not content with the conditions under which they lived, and they put that expression of discontent into the form of a Declaration of Independence, and maintained that declaration with their blood. . . . Discontent under a monarchy may end in despair or it may end in revolution. Discontent under our form of government ends in reform through the peaceful means of the ballot.

Life and Speeches, pp. 313-314.

Ballot Avoids Dam of Public Opinion

In republics, as in other forms of government, there will at times be disturbances, but these come from a failure to recognize and respect the current of public opinion. If we stand by the side of a stream and watch it glide past us, we can in safety listen to the song of the waters, but if we attempt to dam the stream we find the water rising above the dam. If we make the dam still higher, the water rises still more, and at last the force in the obstructed stream is so great that no dam made by human hands can longer live in the valley below, but the fault is not in the stream, but in those who attempt to obstruct it. So in human society there is a current of public opinion which flows ever onward. If left to have its way it does not

harm anyone, but if obstructed, this current may become a menace.   At last
the obstruction must yield to the force of the current.   In monarchies and
aristocracies the dam is sometimes built so high that it is removed by force,
but in republics the ballot can be relied upon to keep the channel of the
stream open, or if obstruction is attempted, to remove it while yet it can be
removed with safety.

Old World, p. 491.

Radical and Conservative Necessary

Both the affirmative and the negative are necessary. You find everywhere the radical and the conservative. Both are essential in a progressive
state. The conservative is necessary to keep the radical from going too far,
and the radical is necessary to make the conservative go at all. One is as
necessary to the welfare of the nation as the other. There must be a party
in power, and there must be a party out of power, altho I think that, for
convenience sake, they ought to change places occasionally.

Speeches, Vol II, p. 208.

Common Right and Divine Right

They are the two principles that have stood the test since the beginning
of time, and they will ever continue to struggle. The one is the common
right of humanity, and the other is the divine right of kings. It is the same
principle in whatever shape it develops itself.

Our reliance is in the love of liberty which God hath planted in our
bosoms. Our defense is the preservation of the spirit which prizes liberty
as the heritage of all men, in all hands everywhere. Destroy this spirit
and you have planted the seed of despotism around your doors.

Commoner, Vol I, p. 27.

Conscience and Heart

Chain the conscience, bind the heart, and you can not have for the
support of our form of government the strength and the enthusiasm it deserves.
But let conscience be free to commune with its God, let the heart be free to
send forth its love, and the conscience and the heart will be the best de-
fenders of a government resting upon the consent of the governed.

Commoner, Vol III, p. 104.

Democracy World Power

Tell me you want to be a world power? Why, for more than ten decades
this nation has been the most potent influence in the world; for more than
a hundred years this nation has done more to affect the politics of the human
race than all the other nations of the world put together. Here you have
witnessed the triumph of an idea. During the closing years of the eighteenth
century this republic was formed; it was dedicated to the doctrine that all
men are created equal; that they are endowed with inalienable rights; that
governments are instituted to secure those rights, and that governments derive their just powers from the consent of the governed. During the nine-
teenth century this idea has grown. Ah, my friends, this idea has been more
powerful than all the armies and all the navies of all the monarchies of the
earth.

Life and Speeches, p. 82.

Majority and Minority

We are asked to change this rule, which has been in operation since
the beginning of the Government, and adopt a new rule - a rule not intended
to enable the majority to rule, but to enable less than one-half of the members of Congress to pass laws for this country. I believe that the innovation
is a dangerous one. There is far more safety in giving to the minority the
power to delay legislation until a majority have expressed themselves in favor
of a law. How can you tell that the people of the United States desire a
particular law except by the voice of their representatives? And how can we
tell that their representatives believe the bill should become a law until
they have expressed themselves by vote in favor of the proposition?

Life and Speeches, p. 46.

Greatest Good for Greatest Number

....the efforts of the Commoner have been to hew close to the line
of what its editor believes to be in the public interests and to faithfully
champion those principles which give the highest promise of providing "the
greatest good to the greatest number".

Commoner, Vol V, p. 1.

Democracy Spreading

The democratic idea is growing - the term is not used in a partisan
sense, but in that broader sense in which it describes government by the

people. There is not a civilized nation in which the idea of popular
government is not growing, and in all the semi-civilized nations there are
reformers who are urging an extension of the influence of the people in
government. So universal is this growth of democratic ideas that there can
be no doubt of their final triumph. Monarchies, at first unlimited, are
now limited, and limited monarchies are recognizing more and more the right
of the people to a voice in their own government.

Old World, p. 490.

Democracy Voice of the People

When the seed, planted in the earth, sends forth the tender leaf and
then the stalk; when the grain appears upon the stalk and supplies the bread
necessary for the support of our bodies, we know that there is back of the
seed a force irresistible and constantly working. As irresistible and as
ceaseless in its activity is the force behind political and moral truth.
The advocates of the American theory of government can, therefore, labor
with the confident assurance that the principles planted upon American soil
a century and a quarter ago are destined to grow here and everywhere until
arbitrary power will nowhere be known, and, until the voice of the people
shall be recognized, if not as the voice of God, at least, as Bancroft defines
it, as the best expression of the divine will to be found upon the earth.

Old World, p. 490.

Government Monopoly Over Private Monopoly

While local considerations and local conditions have much to do in the
determination of each case, there is one general principle which is becoming
more and more clearly outlined as the question of government ownership is
discussed, namely, that when a monopoly becomes necessary it must be a government monopoly and not a monopoly in private hands. In other words, the
principle now most familiarly applied is, "competition where competeition is
possible; government monopoly where competition is impossible".

Old World, p. 480.

Authority By Consent of Governed

I appreciate more than words can express the cordial good-will and the
loyal support of the friends to whom I am indebted for the political honors
which I have received. I am especially grateful to those who bear without
humiliation the name of the common people, for they have been my friends when
others have deserted me. I appreciate also the kind words of many who have
been restrained by party ties from giving me their votes. I have been a

hired man for four years, and, now that the campaign is closed, I may be pardoned for saying that as a public servant, I have performed my duty to the best of my ability, and am not ashamed of the record made.

I stepped from private life into national politics at the bidding of my countrymen; at their bidding I again take my place in the ranks and resume without sorrow the work from which they called me. It is the glory of our institutions that public officials exercise authority by the consent of the governed rather than by divine or hereditary right.

Life and Speeches, p. 47.

American Civilization

Civil and religious liberty, universal education and the right to participate, directly or through representatives chosen by himself, in all the affairs of government - these give to the American citizen an opportunity and an inspiration which can be found nowhere else.

Standing upon the vantage ground already gained, the American People can aspire to a grander destiny than has been opened before any other race.

Anglo-Saxon civilization has, by force of arms, applied the art of government to other races for the benefit of Anglo-Saxons; American civilization will, by the influence of example, excite in other races a desire for self-government and a determination to secure it.

Anglo-Saxon civilization has carried its flag to every clime and defended it with forts and garrisons; American civilization will imprint its flag upon the hearts of all who long for freedom.

Life and Speeches, p. 65.

American Destiny

I can conceive of a national destiny surpassing the glories of the present and the past - a destiny which meets the responsibility of today and measures up to the possibilities of the future. Behold a republic, resting securely upon the foundation stones quarried by revolutionary patriots from the mountain of eternal truth - a republic applying in practice and proclaiming to the world the self-evident proposition that all men are created equal; that they are endowed with inalienable rights; that governments are instituted among men to secure these rights, and that governments derive their just powers from the consent of the governed. Behold a republic in which civil and religious liberty stimulate all to earnest endeavor and in which the law restrains every hand uplifted for a neighbor's injury - a republic in which every citizen is a sovereign, but in which no one cares to wear a crown. Behold a republic standing erect while empires all around are bowed beneath the weight of their own armaments - a republic whose flag is loved while other flags are only feared. Behold a republic increasing in population, in wealth, in strength and in influence, solving the problems of civilization and hastening the coming of an universal brotherhood - a republic which shakes thrones and dissolves aristocracies by its silent example and gives light and inspiration to those who sit in darkness. Behold a republic gradually but surely becoming the supreme moral factor in the world's progress and the accepted arbiter of the world's disputes - a republic whose history, like the path of the just, "Is as the shining light that shineth more and more unto the perfect day".

Under Other Flags, pp. 338-339.

CHAPTER

VII

OPINIONS ON DOMESTIC ISSUES

Equality

Great Issue of Day

The great issue at this time is the issue between Man and Mammon, between democracy and plutocracy. All surface questions of national policy, taxation, of regulation and of finance, are but phases of that century long, that world wide struggle between the common people and organized wealth.

And so, in dealing with principles, with finance, with labor problems and all the other questions at issue, we may view them from a moral standpoint and arraign every evil at the bar of public conscience.

Commoner, Vol V, pp. 1-2.

All Share Citizenship

Shall the lover of his country measure his loyalty only by his service as a soldier? No! Patriotism calls for the faithful and conscientious performance of all of the duties of citizenship, in small matters as well as great, at home as well as upon the tented field.

There is no more menacing feature in these modern times than the disinclination of what are called the better classed to assume the burdens of citizenship. If we desire to preserve to future generations the purity of our courts and the freedom of our people we must lose no opportunity to impress upon our citizens the fact that above all pleasure, above all convenience, above all business, they must place their duty to their government; for a good government doubles every joy, and a bad government multiplies every sorrow. Times change, but principles endure.

Life and Speeches, p. 45.

No Class Privilege

At a meeting held last week in New York to protest against the Wilson bill one of the speakers said: "I traveled through the South and went hundreds of miles without seeing a factory. What do these Southern members know about workingmen? What right have these goose-farmers to make laws for us?"

Why, sir, 58 per cent of the people of the United States live in the country and in villages having a less population than 1000. In the name of those who still believe that "all men are created equal," in the name of those who believe that the harvest hand has the same rights as the hatmaker, and that the farmer is entitled to as much respect as the factory owner, I protest against the arrogant and impudent assumption that it is the privilege of any particular class to make laws for our people, or that any of our citizens, wherever their residence or whatever their occupation, are excluded from an equal voice in the affairs of government.

Life and Speeches, p. 195

No Place for Idle Rich

There is no place in this country for the idle rich, if by that term we mean people who, having acquired money, have no other purpose than to secure all the selfish enjoyment they can out of the use of their money. But there is not only a place, but a crying demand in this country for those who, having acquired enough to relieve themselves from want, will devote themselves to public affairs, It would not be necessary for all of them to hold office. They could contribute their heads and their hearts to their country's service in many ways. They could study public questions and throw their influence upon the side of good government; they could investigate all improvements in the administration of government, and give to the public through addresses and in other ways the benefit of their investigations.

Commoner, Vol III, p. 308.

Use All of One's Ability

The large college furnishes some advantages that the small college can not give; but, my friends, whether we come from large colleges or from small colleges, we come with the same measure of responsibility. God requires much of those to whom much is given, and if our education has made us stronger, we hold that strength as trustees for those who are weaker. If our shoulders are broader, we must put those shoulders under heavier loads.

Commoner, Vol V, pp. 435-436.

Amend Jury Law

While in criminal cases the rule which gives the prisoners the benefit of a reasonable doubt makes it necessary to preserve a unanimous verdict, there is no reason for adhering to it in civil cases.

Under the present requirement, a jury often reports to the judge that it cannot agree, and is sent back with instructions to remain in the jury room until an agreement is reached. In such cases it is little more than a test of endurance. The law should be amended so that 2/3 or 3/4 of a jury may render a verdict.

Commoner, Vol I, p. 74.

Opposed to Court Injunction

The object of the writ is to suspend the right of trial by jury and to give the judge the opportunity to punish for contempt of court in case the order is violated. If the court prohibits the doing of an act already unlawful the order is unnecessary, because those who violate the criminal law can be prosecuted in the ordinary way. If the court prohibits the doing of an act which is not prohibited by law, then it is guilty of creating law, which is not the province of the court.

Commoner, Vol I, p. 400.

Need Unselfish Public Service

There is a crying demand today for unselfish public service. The country needs men of heart and brain who will place a limit on their acquisitions - who after securing a competencey will devote themselves to the betterment of social, economic and political conditions.

Commoner, Vol V, p. 248.

People Purify Politics

The surest way to purify politics is for all the people to give some time, not only to the study of political questions but to attendance upon primaries and conventions and elections. There is enough honesty among the people whenever it is expresses but at present reforms come by spasms rather than by persistent effort.

Commoner, Vol V, p. 248.

No Gifts to Officials

While on the subject of gifts, it may not be out of place to suggest that gifts should not be bestowed upon those who are in official position, for even when they do not suggest an ulterior motive on the part of the donor, they embarrass the recipient. A faithful public servant receives a two-fold reward; his pecuniary compensation satifies any legal obligations he may have against

the community, and the gratitude and appreciation of his constituents fully
settles his account with them.

Commoner, Vol I, p. 343.

Purity in Politics

Purity in politics requires not merely that officials shall keep out of
the penitentiary, but that they shall be above suspicion. If under suspicion
let them step aside until the doubt is removed.

Commoner, Vol II, p. 64.

Corruption Preverted Government

Corruption is the natural and legitimate fruit of the perversion of
government. Only those who are able to make the government a private asset
in business are tempted to contribute largely to campaign funds.

Commoner, Vol V, p. 136.

No Special Privileges

I know of no other plan of campaign today which is so consistent with
our principles, or which offers so much of hope for the party and the people
as the plan followed by Jackson. Taking our stand upon the principle, "Equal
rights to all and special privileges to none", we should declare that wherever
and whenever that principle is attacked we shall resist the attack immediately
and continuously until that principle is applied without question to every
department of the government, national, state and city.

Commoner, Vol V, p. 4.

Political Corruption

The tide is turning. For a quarter of a century corporate influence in
politics has been increasing; campaign funds have grown larger and larger,
and the circle of political corruption has been constantly extended. Voters
were bought; city councils were bribed; state legislatures became the tools
of railroads and monopolies, and the instrumentalities of the federal government were turned to private gain. Three United States senators have been in-
dicted for the misuse of their influence within the last two years, and
officials in high places have been found guilty of plundering the treasury

while drawing salaries from the people.

Commoner, Vol V, p. 12.

Democracy of Heart over Plutocracy of Wealth

I fear the plutocracy of wealth and respect the aristocracy of learning, but I thank God for the democracy of the heart that makes it possible for every human being to do something to make life worth living while he lives and the world better for his existence in it. Mathematicians are able to calculate how far it is from the farthest star to the earth, but no mathematician has yet been able to calculate the influence for good of one kind word, or of one kind act. The life comes into contact with the lives about it, and through this generation it reaches on through the countless generations to come.

Under Other Flags, pp. 261-262.

Against Plutocracy

Plutocracy is abhorrent to a republic; it is more despotic than monarchy, more heartless than aristocracy, more selfish than bureaucracy. It preys upon the nation in time of peace and conspires against it in the hour of its calamity. Conscienceless, compassionless and devoid of wisdom, it enervates its votaries while it impoverishes its victims. It is already sapping the strength of the nation, vulgarizing social life and making a mockery of morals. The time is ripe for the overthrow of this giant wrong.

Speeches, Vol II, p. 91.

Corporate vs. Natural Man

There are many differences between the natural man and the corporate man. There is a difference in the purpose of creation. God made man and placed him upon His footstool to carry out a divine decree; man created the corporation as a money making machine. When God made man He did not make the tallest man much taller than the shortest, and He did not make the strongest man much stronger than the weakest; but when the law creates the corporate person that person may be an hundred, a thousand, ten thousand, a million times stronger than the God-made man. When God made man He set a limit to his existence, so that if he was a bad man he could not be bad long; but when the corporation was created, the limit on age was raised, and it sometimes projects itself through generation after generation

When God made man He gave to mankind a soul and warned him that in the next world he would be held accountable for the deeds done in the flesh; but when man created the corporation he could now endow that corporation with a soul, so that if it escapes punishment here it need not fear the hereafter. And this man-made giant has been put forth to compete with the God-made man.

Speeches, Vol II, pp. 409-410.

Protection Against Corporations

Corporations are the creatures of law and they must not be permitted to pass from under the control of the power which created them; they are permitted to exist upon the theory that they advance the public weal and they must not be allowed to use their powers for the public injury. The right of the United States government to regulate interstate commerce cannot be questioned and the necessity for the vigorous exercise of the right is becoming more and more imperative. The interests of the whole people require such an enlargement of the powers of the interstate commerce commission as will enable it to prevent discrimination between persons and places and protect patrons from unreasonable charges.

Commoner, Vol V, p. 32.

Trusts

Private Monopoly: Indefensible

I want to start with the declaration that a momopoly in private hands is indefensible from any standpoint and intolerable. I make no exceptions to the rule. I do not divide monopolies in private hands into good monopolies and bad monopolies. There is no good monopoly in private hands. There can be no good monopoly in private hands until the Almighty sends us angels to preside over the monopoly. There may be a despot who is better than another despot, but there is no good despotism. One trust may be less harmful than another. One trust magnate may be more benevolent than another, but there is no good monopoly in private hands, and I do not believe it is safe for society to permit any man or group of men to monopolize any article of merchandise or any branch of industry.

Life and Speeches, p. 115.

Competition, Not Trusts

Today I present another demand made in our party platform - the demand that the grip of the trusts be broken, that competition be stored and that the door of opportunity be opened to the business men and the toilers of the land.

Industrial independence is necessary to political independence. The free exercise of the rights of citizenship is impossible when a few men control the industries in which millions are employed.

This question should be settled now; we cannot afford to bequeath it as a legacy of woe to a succeeding generation. The conscience of the people is already awakened, and the conscience is the most potent force of which man has knowledge. Where law makes one righteous, conscience controls a hundred; where one is kept from wrong-doing by fear of prison doors, conscience rears about us - barriers which are stronger than walls of granite. It is upon the conscience that human institutions rest, and without a stirring of the conscience no great reform is possible.

Speeches, Vol II, pp. 141-142.

Encroachments of Trusts

Nearly all of the great lines of industry are being absorbed by the trusts and the lines of transportation are being consolidated until a handful of men practically control the freight and passenger traffic of the nation.

Commoner, Vol V, p. 134.

Creeping Trusts

We find that the natural resources of the country are gradually passing into the hands of a smaller and smaller percentage of the people. The trusts not only plan to exterminate the small competitor, but they are tightening their grip upon the wholesale and retail dealer. . . . and, while they are oppressing the dealer and extorting from the consumer, they are conspiring to destroy the organizations formed by the laboring man for the protection of his rights.

Commoner, Vol V, p. 133.

Rockefeller on Trusts

We are indebted to the younger Rockefeller for an illustration which makes this distinction clear. In defending the trust system he is quoted as saying that the American Beauty Rose cannot be brought to perfection without pinching off ninety-nine buds, so that the one hundredth bud can receive the full strength of the bush, so great industrial organizations are impossible without the elimination of the smaller ones. It is a cruel illustration, but it presents a perfectly accurate picture of trust methods.

Commoner, Vol VI, p. 137.

Tendencies of Trusts

First, the inevitable tendency of a monopoly is to raise the price of the product.

Second, the tendency of a trust is to reduce the price of the raw material used by the trust.

Third, the natural tendency of a trust is to so arbitraily fix the terms and conditions of labor as to take advantage of the laborer, as well as the consumer of the finished product and the producer of the raw material.

Fourth, the natural tendency of a trust is to produce an inferior article. Where there is competition the effort of each competitor is directed toward the furnishing of the best quality at the lowest price, and under this system we have seen reputations established and the character of good so fixed that the stamp of the maker gave added value to the product.

Fifth, the trust does injustice to competitors. When there is competition between a number of corporations or individuals, and when a monopoly is prohibited, no one of them will attempt to employ against the others the usual method now in vogue - namely, underselling in one section while the price is kept up in other sections.

Sixth, another evil that has grown up with the trusts is the freezing our of the small stockholders.

Seventh, one of the far-reaching effects of the trust is to discourage the man ambitious for independence, and when this discouragement becomes permanent and wide-spread, it will mean a tremendous loss in the productive energy of the country.

Commoner, Vol V, pp. 122-123.

Natural Rights vs. Corporate Rights

The natural man has inalienable rights - rights which the government did not give, rights which the government can not take away - the corporation has no rights which the government did not give and no rights which the government can not take away when the welfare of society requires it.

Commoner, Vol V, p. 130.

Awakening Against Greed

I ask you if it is not time to appeal to the ideals that we know are in men? We in this country are sharing in the great world-wide ethical awakening. We today are finding an increasing number of men who are beginning to ask how far greed is going to go. Is it not time that the newspapermen began to search themselves and examine their conduct, and decide where they are going to stand in this ethical movement?

Commoner, Vol VI, p. 155.
At Newspapermen's Dinner, New York City.

Remedy Power of Wealth

Now, we have to act up to our responsibilities. We see in this country the encroachments of wealth. I care not who is to blame. It is not so much our duty to find out who did it as to find a remedy for it. A man asked me the other day why some of the men who have been very bitter in opposing our ideas have changed their views, and my reply was that people who live in a valley are apt to watch the dams above them, for they know that if a flood comes the higher the dam the greater the destruction. Gentlemen, you have been damming the tide of public opinion, and the sooner you remedy the abuses the less radical will be the remedies applied.

Commoner, Vol VI, p. 157.
At Newspapermen's Dinner, New York City.

Government Ownership

As to the right of the government, federal and state, to own and operate railroads there can be no doubt. If we can deepen the water in lakes and build connecting canals in order to cheapen railroad transportation during half of the year, we can build a railroad and cheapen rates in the whole of the year; if we can spend several hundred millions on the Panama Canal to lower transcontinental rates, we can build a railroad from New York to San Francisco to lower both transcontinental and local rates.

Commoner, p. 137.

Labor

Wealth Created by Laborers

I am going to talk today to business men, and I want to say to you that in pleading the cause of the farmer and laborer I am trying to lay a substantial foundation upon which the business of this country can be done. If you engage in merchandise and in the exchange of wealth and suppose that the prosperity of the producer depends upon you you deceive yourselves. Wealth must be created before it can be distributed. Those who create wealth could live although you should go out of business, but you cannot live if the producers of wealth go out of business. I believe that the policy is best for this country which brings prosperity first to those who toil. Give them first the inspiration to work and then protect them in the enjoyment of their rightful share of the proceeds of their toil, and their prosperity will find its way up to the other classes of society which rests upon them. I challenge you to find in the pages of recorded history a single instance where prosperity came from the upper crust of society. It always comes from the masses - the foundation of society.

Life and Speeches, p. 340.

Dignity of Labor

One thought has grown upon me as we have traveled, namely, the dignity
of labor. In no other country is so high an estimate placed upon the wage-
earner as in this country. In the Orient there was, until the advent of
western ideas, an impassable gulf between the prince and his people, and
there is even now in a large part of Asia a gulf so wide that one who toils
with his hands cannot look across it. The royal families have lived by
the sword and they have forced from those beneath them a tribute sufficient
to support themselves and their armed retainers. The masses have been the
prey of the governing classes, no matter what tribe or family held the throne.

Old World, p. 483.

Progress of Laborer in Europe

In Europe it is a question between labor and capital and the laborer
is organizing for the advancement of his welfare. The guild and the labor
organization have long sought to enlarge the laborer's share of the joint
profit of labor and capital and to improve the conditions which form his
environment. The efforts of these societies have mainly been directed, first,
toward the improvement of sanitary conditions; second, toward the shortening
of hours; and third, toward an increase in wages. It looks like a reflection
on mankind in general to say that laboring men should have to ask legislation
to protect their lives while at work

Old World, p. 482.

Natural Rights of All

The first thing that is needed for a better understanding of labor
questions is the recognition of the equal rights of all, and , second,
more intimate acquaintance. We have rights that may be called natural
rights; they are inherent; we have them because we are human beings. The
government did not bestow them upon us - the Government cannot rightfully
withdraw them from us. We all come into the world without our volition;
the environment of youth largely determines the course of our lives, and
this environment is not of our choosing. We live under the same moral
obligations, and are responsible to the same Supreme Being. We have our
needs that must be supplied; we require food, clothing, shelter, compan-
ionship. We have our domestic ties, and the tenderness of these ties is not
measured by wealth or position in society. Man has used petty distinctions
to separate society into different classes, but these distinctions are in-
significant when compared with the great similarities that unite us in a
common destiny and impel us toward a common end.

On this day it is well to emphasize the fact that we are linked together by bonds which we could not break if we would and should not weaken if
we could.

Speeches, Vol II, p. 166-167.

Rights of Labor

In dealing with the labor question, the recognition of equal rights to all is essential. The right of the laboring man to a trial by jury is as sacred as the right of other members of society to a trial before a jury of peers. This right is denied by government by injunction. The right of laboring man to reasonable hours ought to be observed as sacredly as the right of other members of society to reasonable hours. If we recognize as we do the necessity for hours of recreation for ourselves and families, we ought not to begrudge these hours to those who toil at less pleasant and more fatiguing work. If we desire an income that will relieve our children from the necessity of labor while they are young, we should not forget that the laborer has the same interest in his children and that society, too, has a right to demand that they should be so cared for and so educated that they cam, when grown, give to their country the highest and most efficient service.

Under Other Flags, pp. 271-272.

Equal Rights

Those who claim the right to arbitrarily determine the hours, the wages and the conditions of labor demand the right to arbitrarily determine the status of the laboring man and to fix the conditions that are to surround him and his posterity. Is it an interference with property rights to demand that the laboring man shall have a fair share of the proceeds of his own toil - a fair share of the property which he creates? His right to accumulate property should not be ignored. Not only should he be allowed to accumulate property, but he should have leisure to enable him to enjoy communion with his own family and to fit himself for intelligent participation in the affairs of his government. By what authority will t.ə capitalist put his claim to larger dividends above the rights of the wage earners, and the welfare of the wage earner's children?

Commoner, Vol V, p. 206.

Dignity of Labor

Let me go a step farther and appeal for a clearer recognition of the dignity of labor. The odium which rests upon the work of the hand has exerted a baneful influence the world around. The theory that idleness is more honorable than toil - that is more respectable to consume what others have produced than to be a producer of wealth - has not only robbed society of an enormous sum, but it has created an almost impassable gulf between the leisure classes and those who support them. Tolstoy is right in asserting that most of the perplexing problems of society grow out of the lack of sympathy between man and man. Because some imagine themselves above work, while others see before them nothing but a life of drudgery, there is constant warring and much of bitterness.

Speeches, Vol II, pp. 220-22

Opposed to Government by Injunction

The laboring men are seeking relief from government by injunction. Wh;
Because it is employed by corporations to deprive their employees of the
right to trial by jury. If a man is accused of larceny or assault he is en
titled to a trial by jury, why should this right be denied a laboring man
when he is accused of interfering with his employer's business?

Commoner, Vol IV, p. 74.

Reforms Interrelated

Reforms advance in groups. It is seldom that one real reform is
achieved alone, so the limitation of hours of labor has, as a rule, accompanied legislation for the protection of children and for the improvement
of sanitary conditions in mines and workshops. Those who now enjoy an
eight-hour day can remember the nine-hour day and the ten-hour day, but
can hardly recall the days of twelve and fourteen hours.

Old World, p. 482

Arbitration Through Equal Rights

At this time, one of the most important questions in connection with
labor is the question of arbitration, and it is becoming more and more
apparent that a peaceful adjustment of the differences between corporations
and their employees is as necessary to the welfare of society at large as
it is to the laboring man. There is no more reason why a laboring man
should be compelled to fight out his differences with his employer by strik
or boycott than there is for compelling citizens to abandon courts of
justice and settle their differences with each other personally. "Equal
rights to all and special privileges to none" must therefore be observed
in the settlement of the problems that affect employee and employer.

Under Other Flags, p. 272.

Arbitration Good for Society

I believe in arbitration. The principle is not new; it is simply an extension of the court of justice. Arbitration provides an impartial tribunal before which men may settle their differences instead of resorting to violence. New conditions necessitate new laws. . . . Arbitration is not only good for employer and employee, but is necessary for the security of society. Society, has, in fact, higher claims than either employer or employee. The whole people are disturbed by the conflicts between labor and capital, and the best interests of society demand that these differences shall be submitted to and settled by courts of arbitration rather than by trials of strength.

Life and Speeches, p. 315.

Protection for Depositor

Why not make the depositor secure? The United States Government requires the deposit of specific security when it entrusts money to a national bank, altho it can examine the bank at any time; the State requires security when it deposits money in a bank; the country requires security and the city requires security, even the banks require security from the officials who handle money. Why should the depositor be left to take his chances?

Not only is the depositor without protection, but the security given to nation, state, county and city lessens his security. They are preferred creditors; they have a mortgage on the gilt-edged assets and the depositor must get along as best he can with what remains. Why are the interests of depositors thus neglected?

Speeches, Vol II, p. 143.

Opposed to Repeal of Sherman Act

The President of the United States, in the discharge of his duty as he sees it, has sent to Congress a message calling attention to the present financial situation, and recommending the unconditional repeal of the Sherman law as the only means of securing immediate relief. Some outside of this hall have insisted that the President's recommendation imposes upon Democratic members an obligation, as it were, to carry out his wishes, and overzealous friends have even suggested that opposition to his views might subject the hardy dissenter to administrative displeasure. They do the President great injustice who presume that he would forget for a moment the independence of the two branches of Congress. He would not be worthy of our admiration, or even respect, if he demanded a homage which would violate the primary principles of free representative government. . . .

Yes, Mr. Speaker, it is before the tribunal established by our constituencies, and before that tribunal only, that we must appear for judgment upon our actions here. When we each accepted a commission from 180,000 people we pledged ourselves to protect their rights from invasion and to reflect their wishes to the best of our ability, and we must stand defenseless before the bar if our only excuse is, "He recommended it".

Life and Speeches, p. 138.

Broad Definition of Businessman

We say to you that you have made the definition of a businessman too limited in its application. The man who is employed for wages is as much a businessman as his employer; the attorney in a country town is as much a businessman as the corporation counsel in a great metropolis; the merchant at the crossroads store is as much a businessman as the merchant of New York; the farmer who goes forth in the morning and toils all day - who begins in the spring and toils all summer - and who by the application of brain and muscle to the natural resources of the country creates wealth, is as much a businessman as the man who goes upon the board of trade and bets upon the price of grain; the miners who go down a thousand feet into the earth, or climb two thousand feet upon the cliffs, and bring forth from their hiding places the precious metals to be poured into the channels of trade are as much businessmen as the few financial magnates who, in a back room, corner the money of the world. We come to speak for this broader class of business-men.

Memoirs, p. 104.

New Era of Business

It is upon the conscience that human institutions rest, and without a steering of the conscience no great reform is possible, to a national con-science already aroused we appeal, with the pledge that a democratic victory will mean the ringing out of industrial despotism and the ringing in of a new era in which business will be built upon its merits and in which men will succeed, not in proportion to the propaganda they may be able to practice, but in proportion to their industry, their ability and their fidelity.

Speeches, Vol II, p. 141.

President Jackson Reduced Bank Power

When General Jackson was informed that the British had landed just below New Orleans, he replied, "By the Eternal, they shall now sleep on American soil," and although he was awaiting reinforcements he harassed the enemy so constantly for the next two weeks that in the final struggle

he won an easy victory over an exhausted foe. When the president of the
United States Bank, Nicholas Biddle, attempted to threaten him with the
statement that he, as the head of the bank, had the power to defeat him
or to re-elect him, he answered, "If you have the power, you have a _____
sight more power than any man ought to have in this country," and he proceeded to strip the head of the bank of that power.

Commoner, Vol V, p. 4.

Corrections for Banks' Ills

Why do not these financiers apply the remedy to the diseased part? If
the gentleman from New York (Mr. Hendrix), to whom I listened with pleasure,
and who said, "I have come into this Hall as a banker, I am here as the president of a national bank," desires to restore confidence, let him propose for
the consideration of the members a bill to raise, by a small tax upon deposits,
a sum sufficient to secure depositors against possible loss; or a bill to compel stockholders to put up security for their double liability; or to prevent
stockholders or officers from wrecking a bank to carry on their private business; or to limit the liabilities which a bank can assume upon a given amount
of capital, so that there will be more margin to protect its creditors; or a
bill to make more severe the punishment for embezzlement, so that a man can
not rob a bank of a half-million and escape with five years, and can not be
boarded at a hotel by a marshal, while the small thief suffers in a dungeon.
Let him propose some real relief and this House will be glad to cooperate
with him.

Speeches, Vol I, pp. 128-129.

Support for Conservation of Resources

I begin with the proposition that it should be our purpose, not only to
preserve our Nation's resources for future generations by reducing waste to
the minimum, to see to it that a few of the people do not monopolize that
which is in equity the property of all the people. The earth belongs to
each generation, and it is as criminal to fetter future generations with
perpetual franchises, as it would be to unnecessarily impair the common
store.

Speeches, Vol II, pp. 399-400.

America Worth 2% Income Tax

If we have people who value free government so little that they prefer to live under monarchical institutions, even without an income tax, rather than live under the stars and stripes and pay a 2 per cent tax, we can better afford to lose them and their fortunes than risk the contaminating influence of their presence.

Speeches, Vol I, p. 179.

Tariff Disproportionate Tax

The gentleman forgets that the pending tariff bill will collect upon imports more than one hundred and twenty millions of dollars - nearly ten times as much as we propose to collect from the individual income tax. Everybody knows that a tax upon consumption is an unequal tax, and that the poor man by means of it pays far out of proportion to the income which he enjoys.

Why, sir, the gentleman from New York (Mr. Cockran) said that the poor are opposed to this tax because they do not want to be deprived of participation in it, and that taxation instead of being a sign of servitude is a badge of freedom. If taxation is a badge of freedom, let me assure my friend that the poor people of this country are covered all over with the insignia of freedom.

Speeches, Vol I, pp. 165-166.

False Economy of Opponents of Income Tax

And, Mr. Chairman, I desire here to enter my protest against the false political economy taught by our opponents in this debate and against the perversion of language which we have witnessed. They tell us that it is better to consider expediency than equity in the adjustment of taxation. They tell us that it is right to tax comsumption, and thus make the needy pay out of all proportion to their means, but that it is wrong to make a slight compensation for this system by exempting small incomes from an income tax. They tell us that it is wise to limit the use of necessaries of life by heavy indirect taxation, but that it is vicious to lessen the enjoyment of the luxuries of life by a light tax upon large incomes. They tell us that those who make the load heaviest upon persons least able to bear it are distributing the burdens of government with an impartial hand, but that those who insist that each citizen should contribute to government in proportion as God has prospered him are blinded by prejudice against the rich. They call that man a statesman whose ear is tuned to catch the slightest pulsations of a pocketbook, and denounce as a demagogue anyone who dares to listen to the heart-beat of humanity.

Speeches, Vol I, pp. 176-177.

Direct Election of Senator

Advantages of Direct Vote

While it may be impossible to secure favorable action at this time, as effort ought to be made in the senate to bring up for consideration a resolution looking to the election of the United States senator by a direct vote of the people.

Whatever causes may have led to the adoption of the existing method of selecting senators, experience has not only shown that the people can be trusted with the direct choice of their public servants, but it has also demonstrated that the nearer the government is brought to the voters the better it is for both the government and the people. There is more virtue in the masses than ever finds expression through their representatives, because representatives are influenced, to a greater or lesser extent, by their personal interests.

Commoner, Vol I, p. 21.

One Term Presidency

Resolution for One-Term Consitutional Amendment

"Resolved, that we favor a constitutional provisions limiting the office of President and Vice-President to one term, and providing for the election of senators of the United States by a direct vote of the people."

Mr. Bryan - Mr. Speaker, I understand that that is in the Populist Platform, and I do not think it makes the proposition any worse because it was embodied in that platform. The platform adopted by my congressional convention also declared in favor of the election of senators by a direct vote. The proposition is good, it matters not who advocates it. It is good whether the Democrats advocate it or whether the Republicans advocate it or whether the Populists advocate it. It is good because it is consistent with "a government of the people, by the people and for the people," and I welcome it whether it comes from the Populist platform or from any other source, or whether it comes without the endorsement of any convention.

Life and Speeches, p. 304.

Fifty-Third Congress Avoided One-Term Resolution

The determination to hold the office for but one term, in case of election, was not hastily formed. For several years past I have believed that the Federal Constitution should be so amended as to make the President ineligible for re-election.

During the Fifty-Third Congress, I introduced a resolution providing for the submission of such an amendment. A favorable report was made, but I was unable to secure its consideration.

Life and Speeches, p. 363.

Disclaims Possible Second Term

So deeply am I impressed with the magnitude of the power enacted by the constitution in the chief executive of the nation and with the enormous influence which can be yielded for the benefit of injury of the people; that I wish to enter the office, if elected free from every personal desire except a desire to prove worthy of the confidence of my countrymen. Human judgment is fallible enough when unbiased by selfish considerations, and, in order that I may not be tempted to use the patronage of the office to advance any personal ambition, I hereby announce, with all the emphasis which words can express, my fixed determination, not under any circumstances, to be a candidate for re-election in case this campaign results in my election.

Commoner, Vol IV, p. 347.

Opposed Second Term for Himself

The editor of the Commoner has for a number of years urged a constitutional amendment which would make the president ineligible to re-election. He introduced a resolution when a member of congress proposing such an amendment, and in both of his campaigns announced his fixed purpose, if elected, not to be a candidate for re-election.

Commoner, Vol IV, p. 195.

Vice-President Should be Informed

According to the Constitution the vice-president succeeds to the office in case the president dies, resigns, is removed, or becomes unable to discharge the duties of the office. The public good requires that he should be thoroughly informed as to the details of the administration and made ready to take up the work of the executive at a moment's notice. The vice-president ought to be ex-officio and a member of the president's cabinet; he ought to sit next to the president in the council chamber.

Commoner, Vol I, p. 5.

Universal Suffrage

Political Value of Suffrage

Be not frightened; time and again in history the timid have been afraid. But they have always found that they underestimated the number of those who had not bowed the knee to Baal. The Bible tells us of a time when the Elisha was told by his servant that the enemy was too great for them, the prophet answered: "Fear not, they that be with us are more than they that be against us". And then he drew aside the veil and on the mountain top the young man could see horses and chariots that had been invisible before. In just a few days another state will ratify the Suffrage Amendment, and then on the mountain tops you will see the women and children, our allies in every righteous cause. We shall not fail.

Memoirs, p. 473.

Woman's Suffrage

The child is the treasure of the mother; she invests her life in her child. When the mother of the Gracchi was asked: "Where are your jewels?" she pointed to her sons. The mother's life trembles in the balance at the child's birth, and for years it is the object of constant care. She expends upon it her nervous force and energy; she endows it with the wealth of her love. She dreams of what it is to do and be - and, O, if a mother's dreams only came true, what a different world this would be! The most pathetic struggle that this earth knows is not the struggle between armed men upon the battlefield; it is the struggle of a mother to save her child when wicked men set traps for it and lay snares for it. And as long as the ballot is given to those who conspire to rob the home of a child it is not fair - no one can believe it fair - to tie a mother's hands while she is trying to protect her home and save her child. If there is such a thing as justice, surely a mother has a just claim to a voice in shaping the environment that may determine whether her child will realize her hopes or bring her gray hairs in sorrow to the grave.

Because God has planted in every human heart a sense of justice, and because the mother argument makes an irresistible appeal to this universal sense, it will finally batter down all opposition and open women's pathway to the polls.

Memoirs, p. 506.

Cross of God

It is the issue of 1776 over again. Our ancestors, when but three millions in number, had the courage to declare their political independence of every other nation; shall we, their descendants, when we have grown to seventy millions, declare that we are less independent than our forefathers? No, my friends, that will never be the verdict of our people. Therefore, we care not upon what lines the battle is fought. If they say bimetallism is good, but that we can not have it until other nations help us, we reply that, instead of having a gold standard because England has, we will restore bimettallism, and then let England have bimetallism because the United States has it. If they dare to come out into the open field and defend the gold standard as a good thing, we will fight them to the uttermost. Having behind us the producing masses of this nation and the world, supported by the commercial interests, the laboring interests, and the toilers everywhere, we will answer their demand for a gold standard by saying to them: "You shall not press down upon the brow of labor this crown of thorns, you shall not crucify mankind upon a cross of gold."

Memoirs, pp. 498-499.

Decide For or Against Gold

If the gold standard is good, let it be indorsed; if it is bad, the party cannot afford to be silent about it. No half-way measures will do; either the financiers will be given control, not only of the financial system of the country, but of the entire government, or the government must be placed in the hands of those who will administer it in the interest of the masses.

Commoner, Vol II, pp. 197-198.

Racial Attitude

Superior and Inferior Races

Unless all arguments in favor of civilization are without foundation, the superior race, of dominant, would be more considerate toward the inferior race than the inferior race would,if dominant, be toward the superior race. A superior race, when dealing with an inferior one (where it is necessary that one shall be dominant), is restrained, first, by its conscience, and, second, by its view of its own interests; and it is only fair to assume that the superior race will be more responsive to the dictates of conscience and will take a broader view of its own interests, than an inferior race will.

To make the application, the white people of the south, if in control, will be more apt to deal justly with the blacks than the blacks would be, if in control, to deal justly with the whites. And the whites, if in control, will be more amenable to public opinion and will take a more comprehensive view of their own interests than the blacks would if in the same position. People differ not so much in the possession of a selfish spirit as they do in their breadth of view when they consider their own interests. The man who steals is selfish, and yet the man who refrains from stealing takes better care of his own interests than the man does who steals. If the white people of the south make laws that are unjust to the blacks, the more intelligent blacks will leave the south, and the whites of the south will suffer because of the absence of a refining and elevating element among the blacks. The provision which the white people of the south have, at heavy expense, made for the education of the negro, shows that they realize that it is to their interest to raise the standard and elevate the condition of the black man. The excesses of the black legislatures after the war show, on the other hand, the indifference of the blacks to their own interests as well as to the interests of the white people.

Commoner, Vol III, pp. 284-285.

Duties of Superior Nations

I take it for granted that our duty to the so called inferior races is not discharged by merely feeding them in times of famine, or by contributing to their temporary support when some other calamity overtakes them. A much greater assistance is rendered them when they are led to a more elevated plane of thought and activity by the ideals which stimulate them to self-development. The improvement of the people themselves should be the paramount object of all intercourse with the Orient.

In India, in the Phillipines, in Egypt and even in Turkey, statistics show a gradual extension of education, and I trust I shall be pardoned if I say that neither the Army nor the Navy, nor yet the commerce of our Nations, have given us so just a claim to the gratitude of the people of Asia, as have our school teachers, sent, many of them, by private rather than public funds.

An idea will sometimes revolutionize an individual, a community, a state, a nation, or even a world, and the idea that man possesses an inalienable right which the state did not give, and which the state, cannot deny, cannot take away, will make millions of humans stand erect and claim their God-given inheritance.

If the superior nations have a mission, it is not to wound, but to heal - not to cast down, but to lift up, and the means must be example - a far more powerful and enduring means than violence. Example may be likened to the sun, whose genial rays constantly coax the buried seed into life, and clothe the earth, first with verdure and after with ripened grain; while violence is the occasional tempest, which can ruin, but cannot give life.

Commoner, Vol IV, p. 73.

All Races Have Inalienable Rights

The position which I take does not in the least controvert the principles set forth in the Declaration of Independence. A qualification for suffrage does not deny the natural and inalienable rights of the black man. The negro in the south, as I have frequently pointed out, has the same constitutional guarantees as the white man, and lives under the law that the white man makes for himself. If he can not vote today, he can look forward to the time when he may vote.

Commoner, pp. 285-286.

Superior Race Must Act for Self-Preservation

Where two races must live together under the same government, the superior race, as a matter of self-preservation, will impose conditions upon the inferior, just as the individual may defend himself even to the point of taking life in the protection of his own life, or he may put a dangerous enemy under bonds to keep the peace. It is not a denial of the equal rights of others to protect one's own right, but as it is always necessary for one to show that he acted for the protection himself, so at the bar of public opinion those who fix suffrage qualifications upon others must show that it is done in self-defense and for self-preservation.

Commoner, Vol III, p. 286.

CHAPTER

VIII

OPINIONS ON FOREIGN ISSUES

Nation's Strength in Principle

The nations that have failed have decayed morally before they have failed physically. If our nation is to endure, it must stand for eternal principles and clothe itself in their strength. There are some who say that we must now have the largest navy in the world to terrorize other nations, and make them respect us. But if we make our navy the largest in the world, other nations will increase their navies because we have increased ours, and then we will have to increase ours again, because they will have increased theirs, and they will have to increase theirs again because we have increased ours - and there is no limit to this rivalry, but the limit of the power of the people to bear the burdens of taxation.

Speeches, Vol II, pp. 259-260.

Tariff

Ideals Freer than Merchandise

The world is coming to understand that armies and navies, however numerous and strong, are impotent to stop thought. Thought inspired by love will yet rule the world. I am glad that there is a national product more valuable than gold or silver, more valuable than cotton or wheat or corn or iron - an ideal. That is a merchandise - if I may call it such - that moves freely from country to country. You cannot vex it with an export tax or hinder it with an import tariff . . . . It is greater than legislators, and rises triumphant over the machinery of government. In the rivalry to present the best ideal to the world, love, not hatred, will control.

Under Other Flags, p. 134.

Politics and Protective Tariff

The "fat-frying" process has become familiar to the American People. Pressure has been brought to bear upon the protected interests every four years - and to a less extent in the congressional campaigns between presidential elections - to compel contributions to the campaign fund in re-

turn for former favors and in anticipation of favors yet to come. It is
difficult to over-estimate the corrupting influences introduced into the
political life of the nation by this partnership between the Government
and the favored industries. The literature circulated in support of a
protective tariff has studiously cultivated the idea that suffrage should
be employed to secure pecuniary returns, and the appeal made by the Republican leaders has come to be more and more a selfish one.

Speeches, Vol I, p. 295.

Need Equally Based Tax

Is it right to tax all of the people for the benefit of a few? Where
a community has attempted to collect taxes for the aid of an industry, even
when the industry was to be located in the community, the highest court in
the land has declared such a tax to be larceny in the form of law. If a
city government cannot rightfully tax all the people to bring an industry
into the city, where such benefits as are conferred are more easily seen
and more universally enjoyed, who will say that a farmer in the Missouri
Valley can be rightfully taxed to support an industry in a distant State?

As a matter of public policy, is it wise that the industries that
do pay should be compelled to carry upon their backs industries which,
according to the arguments made by their representatives, could not live
without aid? Have we not seen this system introducing corruption into
politics, and is it not building business upon an unsubstantial basis?

Speeches, Vol I, pp. 313-314.

Arbitration Practical

The interests of the laboring man and the interests of the public
demand the substitution of arbitration for the clumsy and expensive strike
system and the employers ought to consent to it. An impartial body would
in nearly every case reach a decision acceptable to all and thus avert a
test of endurance. It is not necessary that the finding be binding on the
parties. If there is compulsory submission of the questions in dispute
public opinion can be relied upon to enforce the findings.

Commoner, Vol V, p. 230.

Laborer Owes Society

Having mentioned some of the things which the laboring man has a right
to demand, let me add that society also makes demands upon the laborer. Our
obligations in this life are mutual ones. None of us stand in a position

where we can demand without making return. The laboring man owes faithful services to his employer and the labor organization will commend itself to the employers in proportion as its influence upon the members tends to increase their efficiency.

Commoner, Vol V, p. 266.

Laborers Owe Respect for Law

The members of the labor organization also owe to society a respect for law. No one can afford to be lawless and no one can long expect public sympathy who attempts to substitute force and violence for reason and persuasion in any controversy. The labor organization ought to be swift to punish violations of the law among its members, for such violations, when unpunished, bring odium upon the entire body.

Commoner, Vol V, p. 257.

Employer, Employee, and Society have Equal Responsibility

But if it is unwise to make the employer the sole custodian of the rights and interests of the employees, it is equally unwise to give the employee uncontrolled authority over the rights and interests of the employer. The employees are no more to be trusted to act unselfishly and disinterestedly than the employer. In the zeal to secure a present advantage they may not only do injustice, but even forfeit a large future gain.

Speeches, Vol II, pp. 72-73.

Reduction of Tariff

Surely no one will object to a reduction being made upon articles which come into competition with American manufactures which are sold abroad more cheaply than at home. The American manufacturer who sends his goods to foreign lands, and there, without any protection whatever, competes successfully with the manufacturers of all the world, does not need a high tariff to meet competition in the home market.

The second step in the reduction of the tariff is a "material reduction upon the necessities of life, especially upon goods competing with such American manufactures as are sold abroad more cheaply than at home." At present the articles used by the poor bear a higher rate, ad valorem, than the articles used by the rich. This statement can be verified by an examination of any of the schedules. A tax upon consumption, even when laid with absolute impartiality, bears heaviest upon the poor, because our necessities are much more uniform than our possessions. People do not eat in proportion to their income; they do not wear clothing in proportion to their income; they do not use taxed goods in proportion to the income. . . . It is only fair, therefore, that in an attempt to relieve the people from

the inequities of a high tariff, the poor, who are overburdened, should be
given first consideration. Then, too, a reduction in the tariff on the
necessities of life brings a benefit to all the people, while a reduction
in the tax upon luxuries would benefit but a portion of the people.

Speeches, Vol I, pp. 310-311.

Tariff Law Catches Little Fish, not Big Ones

If the tax on salt is a burden to the domestic consumer, but discrim-
inate between the fish-curer of New England and the farmer of the West who
needs salt to pack his winter's meat or salt his cattle? The trouble is
that the ordinary citizen uses it in small quantities, and therefore makes
no vigorous resistence, while the fish-curer, buying in large quantities,
feels the weight of the duty, and not only demands but secures, relief.
In fact, the whole tariff law is full of evidence that the protective net
differs from the fish net. The latter is so made that the small fish get
away while the big fish are caught, but a protective tariff net is so framed
that the big fish get away and the little fish are caught.

Life and Speeches, p. 189.

For Home Industry

When some young man selects a young woman who is willing to trust her
future to his strong right arm; when they start to build a little home, that
home which is the unit of society and upon which our government and our
prosperity must rest; when they start to build this home, and the man who
sells the lumber reaches out his hand to collect a tariff upon it; the men
who furnish the carpets, table-cloths, knives, forks, dishes, furniture,
spoons, everything that enters into the construction and operation of that
home - when all these stretch out their hands, I say, from every direction
to lay their blighting weight upon that cottage, the Democratic party says,
'Hands off, and let that home industry live.' It is protecting the grandest
home industry that this or any other nation ever had.

Memoirs, p. 497.

Bryan Tariff Bill

When Mr. Bryan was a member of the House of Representatives, he introduced a bill which provided that whenever any federal circuit court should
find that a trust existed in restraint of any article upon which duties are
levied by tariff law, it should be the duty of the court to report the fact
so found to the president specifying each and every such article. It was

then made a duty of the president, upon the receipt of such report, to issue
his proclamation placing each and every such article then imported into the
United States upon the free list, and fixing the time, not exceeding thirty
days from the receipt of the findings of the court, at which such article
or articles should be admitted free of duty.

Commoner, Vol II, p. 195.

Imperialism

America Strong in Ideas and Acts

I want this nation to influence, not the feeble races only but the
strong ones as well; I want it to dominate, not merely inferior races, but
also superior ones. I want this nation to conquer the world, not with its
armies and its navies, but with its ideas. I want this nation to destroy
every throne on earth, not by force or violence, but by showing the world
something better than a throne - a government resting upon the consent of
the governed - strong because it is loved, and loved because it is good.
I want this nation to solve the problems of this generation and by doing
so not only bless our own people, but give life and hope to those who labor
under greater disadvantages than we do.

Under Other Flags, pp. 262-263.

World Looks to America

There is not a nation in this world that isn't looking to this country;
we are giving inspiration to all countries. We have nerved the arm of men
to fight for political and religious liberty....We have helped the world.
Our light shines throughout the world and when we do anything good in this
country for our people it has its influence on hands everywhere.

Commoner, Vol VI, p. 161.

Right to Fight For Liberty

Rights never conflict; duties never clash. Can it be our duty to usurp
political rights which belong to others? Can it be our duty to kill those
who, following the example of our forefathers, love liberty well enough to
fight for it?

Speeches, Vol II, p. 35.

Reason over Force

And so with the nation. It is of age and it can do what it pleases; it can spurn the traditions of the past; it can repudiate the principles upon which the nation rests; it can employ force instead of reason; it can substitute might for right; it can conquer weaker people; it can exploit their lands, appropriate their property and kill their people; but it cannot repeal the moral law or escape the punishment decreed for the violation of human rights.

Speeches, Vol II, p. 38.

Destiny Argument Invalid

The "destiny" argument obliterates all distinction between right and wrong; it assumes that there is somewhere an irresistible force which compels the American people to do what they do not want to do and ought not to do.

The destiny argument justifies grand larceny and wholesale slaughter, provided that they will pay, and then imperialists, conscious that the means employed cannot be defended by argument, throw the blame upon Providence. There is no more reason to believe that God commands a big nation to destroy, subjugate or rob a weaker nation than there is to believe that God commands a strong man to kill or rob a cripple, and yet imperialists invoke the law to punish the individual as a criminal, while they extol a war of conquest as patriotic.

Commoner, Vol I, p. 186.

Imperialism Not Destiny

When the advocates of imperialism find it impossible to reconcile a colonial policy with the principles of our government or with the canons of morality; when they are unable to defend it upon the ground of religious duty or pecuniary profit, they fall back in helpless despair upon the assertion that it is destiny. "Suppose it does violate the constitution," they say; "suppose it does break all the commandments; suppose it does entail upon the nation an incalculable expenditure of blood and money - it is destiny, and we must submit."

The people have not voted for imperialism; no national convention has declared for it; no Congress has passed upon it. To whom, then, has the future been revealed? Whence this voice of authority? We can all prophesy, but our prophesies are merely guesses, colored by our hopes and our surroundings. Man's opinion of what is to be is half wish and half environment. Avarice paints destiny with a dollar mark before it; militarism equips it with a sword.

He is the best prophet who, recognizing the omnipotence of truth, comprehends most clearly the great forces which are working out the progress, not of one party, not of one nation, but of the human race.

Life and Speeches, p. 60.

Ideal Destiny of America

If this nation enters upon a career of imperialism it ceases to be a moral factor in the world's progress. If this nation enters upon a career of conquest it is not in position to raise its protest against that doctrine when applied by other nations.

You ask me what my ideal of this nation's destiny is? I tell you that it is to make this the greatest republic on earth, the greatest republic of history; and then as we grow in strength, in population and in influence, we can raise our voices with increasing emphasis in behalf of truth and justice. I want this nation to stand erect and be able to say at all times that the people in this nation sympathize with anybody who is willing to die for liberty.

Life and Speeches, p. 87.

Opposing Forms of Government

Whether we can govern colonies as well as other countries can is not material; the real question is, whether we can, in one hemisphere, develop the theory that governments derive their just power from the consent of the governed, and, at the same time, inaugurate, support and defend in the other hemisphere a government which derives its authority entirely from superior force.

And if these two ideas of government cannot live together, which one shall we oppose? To defend forcible annexation on the ground that we are carrying out a religious duty is worse than absurd. . . .

But even if we could destroy every vestige of the laws which are the outgrowth of the immortal document penned by Jefferson; if we could obliterate every written word that has been inspired by the idea that this is "a government of the people, by the people and for the people," we could not tear from the heart of the human race the hope which the American republic has planted there. The impassioned appeal, "Give me liberty or give me death," still echoes around the world.

Life and Speeches, pp. 68-69.

Imperialism Un-Christian

If true Christianity consists in carrying out in our daily lives the teachings of Christ, who will say that we are commended to civilize with dynamite and proselyte with the sword? He who would declare the divine will must prove his authority either by Holy Writ or by evidence of a special dispensation. Imperialism finds no warrant in the Bible. The command "Go ye into all the world and preach the gospel to every creature" has no Gatling-gun attachment. When Jesus visited a village of Samaria and the people refused to receive Him some of the disciples suggested that fire should be called down from heaven to avenge the insult, but the Master rebuked them and said: "Ye know not what manner of spirit ye are of, for the Son of Man is not come to destroy men's lives, but to save them." Suppose He had said: "We will thrash them until they understand who we are," how different would have been the history of Christianity! Compare, if you will, the swaggering, bullying, brutal doctrine of imperialism with the golden rule and the commandment, "Thou shalt love thy neighbor as thyself."

Life and Speeches, p. 408.

Netherlands Adjusting Colonial System

The colonial system also comes under one's observation in a trip around the world. The Netherlands have large colonial possessions in the Malay archipelago, but they have been compelled to abandon the culture system - a form of slavery - and there are signs of a political development which will some day make it necessary for Holland to consult the wishes of the people more than she has in the past.

Old World, p. 488.

Colonialism and Republic Antagonistic

The party's position on imperialism has been stated in two national platforms, and I do not see how the party can recede from that position. Colonialism is antagonistic to the principles of a republic, and we cannot stand before the world as the representative of the doctrine that governments derive their just powers from the consent of the governed, and at the same time declare for the permanent holding of distant islands under a government resting purely upon force.

Commoner, Vol V, p. 5.

Imperialism Extended in Philippines, South Africa, and Cuba

But if it were possible to obliterate every word written or spoken in defense of the principles set forth in the Declaration of Independence a war of conquest would still leave its legacy of perpetual hatred, for it was God Himself who placed in every human heart the love of liberty. He never made a race of people so low in the scale of civilization or intelligence that it would welcome a foreign master.

Those who would have this nation enter upon a career of empire must consider the effect of imperialism upon the Filipinos, but they must also calculate its effects upon our own nation. We cannot repudiate the principle of self-government in the Philippines without weakening that principle here.

Lincoln said that the safety of this nation was not in its fleets, its armies, its forts, but in the spirit which prizes liberty as the heritage of all men, in all lands, everywhere, and he warned his countrymen that they could not destroy this spirit without planting the seeds of despotism at their own doors. . . .

In 1896 all parties manifested a lively interest in the success of the Cubans, but now when a war is in progress in South Africa which must result in the extension of the monarchial idea or in the triumph of a republic the advocates of imperialism in this country dare not say a word in behalf of the Boers. Sympathy for the Boers does not arise from any unfriendliness towards England. The American people are not unfriendly toward the people of any nation. This sympathy is due to the fact that, as stated in our platform, we believe in the principles of self-government and reject, as did our forefathers, the claims of monarchy. If this nation surrenders its belief in the universal application of the principles set forth in the Declaration of Independence it will lose the prestige and influence which it has enjoyed among the nations as an exponent of popular government.

Life and Speeches, pp. 394-395.

Spanish-American War

We have reached another crisis. The ancient doctrine of imperialism, garnished from our land more than a century ago, has recrossed the Atlantic and challenged democracy to mortal combat upon American soil.

Whether the Spanish war shall be known in history as a war for liberty or as a war of conquest; whether this nation shall remain a homogeneous republic or become a heterogeneous empire - these questions must be answered by the American people. When they speak, and not until then, will destiny be revealed.

Destiny is not a matter of change; it is a matter of choice.

Life and Speeches, p. 63.

Spanish-American War Must Not Be War of Conquest

History will vindicate the position taken by the United States in the war with Spain. In saying this I assume that the principles which were invoked in the inauguration of the war will be observed in its prosecution and conclusion. If, however, a contest, undertaken for the sake of humanity, degenerates into a war of conquest, we shall find it difficult to meet the charge of having added hypocrisy to greed. Is our national character so weak that we cannot withstand the temptation to appropriate the first piece of land that comes within our reach?

Life and Speeches, p. 59.

Colonialism Defeats Self-Government

Our nation has been for a hundred years the exponent of the doctrine of self-government. It has brought untold good to the world by presenting a new national ideal to mankind. So long as this nation administers the colonial policy it is important to help the call to human liberty.

The moment this country announces to the world that it has amended the Declaration of Independence, it declares that government can in some instances derive their just powers from some other source than the consent of the government, it ceases to be the champion of the doctrine of self-government, and the injury that would be done to the world by modification of this position must be weighed against any good, real or imaginary, that we could confer upon the Filipinos.

Commoner, Vol IV, p. 454.

Imperialism Injures Reputation

But expensive as imperialism is, when measured by dollars and cents the greatest injury is that done to the honor and the reputation of the nation. We cannot sympathize with the oppressed anywhere without being rebuked by the oppressors and we cannot emphasize at home principles that we are violating in the Orient.

Commoner, Vol IV, p. 68.

Cannot Buy People With Title

What is our title to the Philippine Islands? Do we hold them by treaty or by conquest? Did we buy them or did we take them? Did we purchase the people? If not, how did we secure title to them? Were they thrown in with the land? Will the Republicans say that inanimate earth has value but that when that earth is molded by the divine hand and stamped with the likeness of the Creator it becomes a fixture and passes with the soil? If governments derive their just powers from the consent of the governed, it is impossible to secure title to people, either by force or by purchase.

Speeches, Vol II, pp. 32-33.

Majority of Americans for Filipinos

I appreciate also the kindly manner in which you have referred to the way

in which I have tried to express my friendship for the Filipino people.
I do not propose to discuss here political questions, I have not felt that
in these islands I should enter into any disputed question.

Some things I can say with propriety. While you appreciate the manner
in which I have attempted to tell of my friendship of the Filipinos, do not
make the mistake of believing that those who differ from me are not interested in this people. In my country there are two great parties, Republicans
and Democrats. They enter into contests which are strenuous, but in fundamental principles they are both the same.

In two contests I was defeated by the Republicans but I believe as much
in the patriotism of those who voted against me, as I do in the patriotism
of those who fought for me. Those who agreed with me announced a policy for
the Filipinos. Those who opposed me did not. But do not make the mistake of
believing that those others are enemies to the islands. I believe the majority
of all American people without regard to politics or parties, are sincere
well-wishers of the Filipinos. Yes, all.

Commoner, Vol VI, p.43.

Imperialism Ignored in World

Tell me that we are pleading the cause of the Filipinos? No, my friends,
we are pleading the cause of the American people. If the Filipinos were to
die tomorrow the world would go on, but if this nation ceases to be a republic
the light of civilization goes out. To what nation, then, could struggling
humanity look for hope and inspiration? . . . In every contest heretofore
between monarchy and republicanism the American people have expressed
their sympathy. When Greece was struggling to be free Webster and Clay employed their eloquence in defense of a resolution pledging sympathy. When
the Cubans were fighting for their liberty all parties declared the sympathy
of the American people. But what do we find now? We find that when the
English Government is attempting to take from the people of the Boer republic
the right to govern themselves the people who believe in imperialism in this
country dare not say a word to express their sympathy with the people over
there. This is the paralysis that is already creeping over this nation.

Life and Speeches, pp. 84, 87.

Boers

Avoid Joining England Opposing Boers

Must we abandon the self-evident truth that governments derive their
just powers from the consent of the governed? Must we accept imperialism
as an accomplished fact and join the shout for blood and conquest? Our
republic rests upon solid rock and while its principles are revered, it
cannot be overthrown from within or from without.

It is a law divine in its origin, irresistible in its force and eternal in its duration, that wrong doing ultimately destroys wrong doers; no nation or combination of nations is strong enough to evade or resist retributive justice.

The fact that England had extended more than $1,000 per Boer - the per capita wealth of the United States - and has neither been able to purchase them nor to kill them - these facts are immeasurably valuable to people everywhere who want free government for themselves and are content that others should ejoy it also.

Can the American people consent to an alliance which will bring upon our nation either responsibility for wrongs done by the English government or a share of the punishment which must ultimately be inflicted upon wrong doers, whether they be individuals or nations?

England is sowing the wind; she will reap a whirlwind. This nation cannot join hands with her without adopting her policies, and finally sharing in the terrible retribution which will come.

We cannot afford to be "unequally yoked together" with any government which recognizes force as the basis of government or in its administration disregards the doctrine that governments are the creatures, not the masters, of the people.

Commoner, Vol I, p. 368.

Support Boer's Fight for Independence

That a force so small should be able to hold the British army at bay and even retake some of the surrendered places seems too wonderful to be true. Millions here and throughout the world who believe in self-government and deny the right of a strong nation to cast its sovereignty like a net over a weaker people, are watching with intense interest the unequal struggle of the Boers in defense of their independence. If they succeed in forcing a recognition of their republic, their victory will mark the turning point in the recent trend toward imperial ideas and their sacrifices will be of incalculable value to the human race.

Commoner, Vol I, p. 7.

Sympathy for Boers Based on Principles

Sympathy for the Boers does not arise from any unfriendliness toward England; the American people are not unfriendly toward the people of any nation. This sympathy is due to the fact that, we believe in the principles of self-government and reject, as did our forefathers, the claims of monarchy. If this nation surrenders its belief in the universal application of the principles set forth in the Declaration of Independence, it will lose the prestige and influence which it has enjoyed among the nations as an exponent of popular government.

Speeches, Vol II, p. 25-26.

Boers Help Liberty-Loving People

I did on many occasions express the hope that you would succeed in maintaining the independence of the Boer Republic; I did do all in my power to arouse sympathy for your people in your wonderful struggle to retain self-government, but it was not because of personal acquaintance with your people or because of partiality for them as against others. It was rather because I believe that a blow struck for liberty anywhere strengthens liberty everywhere, and that the defeat of any peoples' aspirations for self-government is felt by liberty loving people all over the world. Your burgers were fighting for all republics as well as for their own and they made England's war of conquest so expensive that all republics are now safer from attack from without.

Commoner, Vol IV, p. 359.

India

British Rule in India Despotic

The government of India is as arbitrary and despotic as the government of Russia ever was, and in two respects it is worse. First, it is administered by an alien people, whereas the officials of Russia are Russians. Second, it drains a large part of the taxes out of the country, whereas the Russian government spends at home the money which it collects from the people. A third disadvantage might be named since the czar has recently created a legislative body, whereas England continues to deny to the Indians any form of representative or constitutional government. Under British rule there is no official corruption and the government is probably as impartial as an alien government can be expected to be, but British rule has the defects which are inherent in a colonial policy.

Old World, p. 299.

British Responsible if Indians Cannot Govern Themselves

But why is there a lack of intelligence among the Indians? Have they not had the blessings of British rule for several generations? Why have they not been fitted for self-government? Gladstone, whose greatness of head and heart shed a lustre upon all Europe, said: "It is liberty alone which fits men for liberty. This proposition, like every other in politics, had its bounds; but it is far safer than the counter doctrine,'wait till they are fit.'"

Old World, p. 305

Taxes Not Used Appropriately for Indian Education

It is not scarcity of money that delays the spread of education in India, but the deliberate misappropriation of taxes collected, and the system which permits this disregard of the welfare of the subjects and the subordination of their industries to the supposed advancement of another nation's trade is as indefensible upon political and economic grounds as upon moral grounds. If more attention were given to the intellectual progress of the many people and more regard shown for their wishes, it would not require so many soldiers to compel loyalty to England, neither would it require a large army to preserve peace and order. If agriculture were protected and encouraged and native industries built up and diversified, England's commerce with India would be greater, for prosperous people would buy more than can be sold to India today, when so many of her sons and daughters are like walking shadows.

Old World, p. 306.

Appreciation of Bryan from Indians

We, the children of Hindustan, residing in New York, respectfully approach your noble presence to offer our sincere and hearty thanks on behalf of three hundred million people of India for the great service you have rendered to that country by exposing the falsehood and hypocrisy which characterized the British rule in the Indian empire. That you took the trouble of paying a visit to our afflicted fatherland, made a thorough investigation of the causes of poverty, famine and plague - the normal conditions of the present India. . . . and having discovered the truth about the ingenious methods of British bureaucracy at Calcutta, gave it out with impartiality to the world at large, has greatly touched all the Indians in this country and millions at home, across the continents and oceans.

Commoner, Vol VI, pp. 150-151.

International Arbitration

Plan for Arbitration

Our nation should take the initiative in promoting a system of arbitration so comprehensive that all differences will be submitted to the arbitration court, reserving to each nation the right to refuse to accept the finding if it believes that it effects its honor or integrity. Such a system would make war a remote possibility.

It is possible, however, to provide for the impartial investigation of any international dispute, leaving the final submission to arbitration to be a matter of treaty. The president might be authorized to enter into an agreement to submit any and every international dispute to the Hague court for investigation.

Why not ask Congress for authority to submit all international questions (when an agreement cannot be reached by the parties interested) to an impartial board for investigation and report. The investigation will, in nearly every case, remove the cause of complaint and reconcile the parties.

Commoner, Vol VI, p. 99.

Arbitration Would Reduce War to Minimum

If the leading nations of the world would enter into an agreement to join in the creation of such a board and pledge themselves to submit all disputes to the board for investigation before declaring war the danger of war would be reduced to a minimum. For men have had it in their power to do so much for humanity - will you improve the opportunity?

Commoner, Vol. V, p. 259.

Advantages to Arbitration

I thank this body for the opportunity to say just a word in defense of my part of the resolution. The first advantage then, of this resolution is that it secures an investigation of the facts, and if you can but separate the facts from the question of honor, the chances are one hundred to one that you can settle both the fact and the question of honor without war. There is, therefore, a great advantage in an investigation that brings out the facts, for disputed facts between nations, and between friends, are the cause of most disagreements.

The second advantage of this investigation is that it gives time for calm consideration.

The third advantage of this investigation is that it gives opportunity to mobilize public opinion for the compelling of a peaceful settlement and that is an advantage not to be overlooked. Public opinion is coming to be more and more a power in the world.

Commoner, Vol VI, p. 102.

Arbitration Must Include Senate

The amendment of the treaties was not "a step backward," as President Roosevelt described it, and there is no reason why the friends of arbitration should be discouraged. An absolute monarch, can, of course, act more quickly than executive who is controlled by a constitution and compelled to consult a co-ordinate branch of the government, but speed is not the only thing to be considered. The framers of our government well understood the relative merits of the various forms of government and chose to risk the evils of delay in order to secure the greater safety that comes with popular government. Arbitration transfers the settlement of a question to the decision of foreign nations - and what action demands more serious consideration? To transfer to the president the power to decide such questions without consulting the senate would arouse so much opposition and cause so much uneasiness that the arbitration movement would be likely to be retarded rather than accelerated by the adoption of the president's views. One serious mistake would bring a revulsion of feeling that might jeopardize the cause of arbitration.

It is possible, however, to provide for the impartial investigation of any international dispute, leaving the final submission to arbitration to be a matter of treaty.

Commoner, Vol V, p. 34.

Investigation Board

Last winter you asked for authority to enter into agreements which would be in effect arbitration treaties and the senate (wisely, I believe) refused to surrender the treaty making power. Why not ask congress for authority to submit all international questions (when an agreement can not be reached by parties interested) to an impartial board for investigation and report. Investigation in nearly every case will remove the cause of complaint and reconcile the parties. Questions which a nation might be unwilling to submit to arbitration in advance could be settled by investigation by an impartial international board.

Commoner, Vol V, p. 259.

Reason Not Force

I am still a young man, so young that I hope that in the course of nature I may live to see the time when Nations, instead of training people to kill each other, will recognize that justice, and justice only, can furnish an enduring foundation for a nation, and would be willing that every question in dispute shall be presented for investigation and deliberation, with the idea of settling all questions by reason and not by force. I have such faith in this sense of justice that I believe in the course of time every question will be settled right. If I did not have faith in that sense of justice I could not advocate any reform, for it is only to the sense of justice that God placed in every human heart that we can appeal.

Commoner, Vol VI, p. 83.

International Education

The country can do infinitely more for itself and infinitely more for
the world by educating representatives of foreign nations and sending them
back to apply American principles to their social and political problems
than it can by wars of conquest.

A hundred students educated in the United States and returned to the
nations of the Orient, would do more towards extending our trade and our
civilization than an army of a hundred thousand men. The federal government could well afford to establish a school and educate all the students
that would be sent here from South America and Asia. The cost to the nations
would be small compared with the cost of a single war of conquest, and the
profit would be immeasurably greater.

Commoner, Vol I, p. 329.

All Peoples Similar

I am more and more impressed with the broadening influence of traveling.
As we visit different countries we learn that people everywhere, no matter
what language they speak, or under what form of government they live, are
much the same. We find that the things that we hold in common are more important and more numerous than the smaller things which separate us.

Commoner, Vol VI, p. 8.

CHAPTER

IX

CREDO FOR DEMOCRATIC PARTY

Jefferson on Political Parties

Men, by their constitutions are naturally divided into two parties:
1. Those who fear and distrust the people, and wish to draw all powers
from them into the hands of the higher classes. II. Those who identify
themselves with the people, have confidence in them, cherish them and consider them as the most honest and safe, although not the wisest depository
of the public interests. In every country these two parties exist, and
in every one where they are free to think, speak and write, they will declare themselves. Call them therefore, liberals and serviles, Jacobins
and Ultras, Whigs and Tories, Republicans and Federalists, Aristocrats
and Democrats, or by whatever name you please, they are the same parties
still, and pursue the same object. The last appellation of aristocrats
and democrats is the true one expressing the essence of all.

Commoner, Vol I, p. 93.

Democrat and Aristocrat

But what are the principles for adherence to which we are so denounced?
Look at the word democracy itself, "The rule of the people." That is the
fundamental idea of the party, and a government by the people is the form
which we desire. Contrast this with the form proposed by Hamilton, that
aristocrat who has been represented, during the last campaign, as the em-
bodiment of sagacity, wisdom, and statesmanship. His plan was that the
president should hold office for life, or during good behavior, and that
the governors of the states should be appointed by him. He feared and dis-
trusted the people, chose for his model the English government, and once
declared that Caesar, who had the courage to take and destroy the power
of the people, was the greatest man who had ever lived. Against Hamilton
and the followers the Democratic party has raised and will forever raise,
its voice.

We want no one-man power. The people are equal before the law and are
supreme. They waked this new world from its sleep of ages; they drove the
savage red man toward the setting sun and turned his fertile hunting grounds
into fields of waving grain; they made the mountain torrents turn the mighty
mill wheels; back and forth, the busy shuttles flew to do their bidding.
Armed with the strength of conscious right, they freed themselves from
English oppression. France trembled before them, and Mexico acknowledges
their power. A civil war has been put down by their arms. Their history
covers an hundred years of unparalleled progress; why should we distrust
them now or take from them the power they have so nobly used?

Memoirs, pp. 244-245.

Principles of Democratic Party

The democratic party must stand for democratic ideals and it must apply democratic principles to all questions regardless of the prospect of temporary victory or the danger of temporary defeat.....

The democratic party must stand erect, neither endorsing the wrong nor surrendering the right. It must invite the confidence of those who want good government and are willing to have the government administered for the benefit of the whole people. Instead of trying to make the democratic party so much like the republican party that we shall get a few republicans by mistake let us make it so different from the republicans who turn from the mammon-serving leaders of that party and seek a party that puts the man before the dollar. When we gain such recruits the party will be strengthened both in numbers and in purpose.

Commoner, Vol III, pp. 48-49.

Position of Democratic Party

The democratic party cannot change its principles to suit the purposes of those reorganizers unless it becomes so similar to the republican party that, so far as the patriotic voter is concerned, there will be small choice between the two organizations. There is but one position for the democratic party to take. It is the plainly defined democratic position. It is the position on the side of the people as clearly defined in the conscience of every thoughtful man.

Commoner, Vol III, p. 91.

Party Must Avoid Temporary Success

And so with party, good character is habitual righteousness. A party suffers whenever it departs from its principles in the hopes of winning a temporary success. The result usually is that it not only fails to win the success-the winning of which it puts above all other things-but that it loses time that ought to have been employed in the work of education. A man must be consistent, and a necessity of consistency in a party is no less imperative.

Commoner, Vol IV, p. 437.

Morality of Party

Our fight must be made upon a moral plane, for we seek justice. Our people must appeal to the conscience of the country, and that conscience

awakened will sweep everything before it. We cannot fight upon a moral plane
with an immoral organization; we cannot appeal to the conscience of the country with a conscienceless crowd in charge of the party machinery. It is absolutely necessary, therefore, that the organization shall be in the hands
of those who are in sympathy with the party's purpose and whose records will
not give the lie to the party's promises.

Commoner, Vol II, p. 64.

Right over Expediency

"The dictionary ought to define political foresight as 'faith in the
wisdom of doing right.' What a contrast between the candid recognition of
the triumph of truth and the miserable and shortsighted doctrine of expediency!

There is no basis upon which one can calculate expediency; there is a
standard of morality and conscience by which one can measure every public
question. One seeks for expediency as the hunter searches for game, uncertain where he will find it. But as the farmer follows his plow, confident that the seed and soil will reward his industry and the earth will
yield its increase, so he who attaches himself to a truth knows that he
works in harmony with immutable and irresistible law.

Let the hosts of democracy take courage; let them appeal to the honest
and conscientious...and put their trust in that sense of justice which is
at once the source and the guarantee of good government.

We may well adopt as a Democratic prayer, and it is a prayer fit for
any party, "Oh God, give us faith in the wisdom of doing right."

Commoner, Vol IV, p. 3.

Voters Should Control Party

Let each democrat pledge himself to attend all of the primaries of his
party to be held between now and the next democratic national convention,
unless unavoidably prevented, and to use his influence to secure a clear,
honest and straightforward declaration of the party's position on every
question upon which the voters of the party desire to speak.

This plan does not involve the writing of a platform in advance of the
primaries; it does not rest upon the paramount importance of any one issue.
It recognizes the right of the democratic voters to control the policy of
the democratic party, and to determine its position upon public question.
It also recognizes the importance of honesty and sincerity in politics.

Commoner, Vol V, p. 61.

Power of Primaries

The pledge proposed is a primary pledge - because the people speak at the primaries. The national convention is attended by delegates and each delegate represents tens of thousands of democrats. The state convention is also attended by delegates, and these represent thousands of democrats. At the primary the voters speak for themselves; there democracy has its citadel.

Commoner, Vol V, p. 62.

Democrats Should Avoid Republican Methods

In some places I found that Democrats were imitating republican methods. They excused it by saying that they were fighting the devil with fire. This is no excuse. It is poor policy to fight the devil with fire. He knows more about fire than you do and does not have to pay so much for fuel.

Speeches, Vol II, p. 252.

Democrats Must Support Principles Above Party

The New York World intimates that the democratic party is dying and the reasons for this impression are stated as follows:

"William Jennings Bryan, twice candidate for president on the democratic ticket, tenders to Mr. Roosevelt his sympathetic support in the campaign of regulating corporations in general and railway rates in particular." . . . .

If democrats are not sufficiently sincere and patriotic to support their own plans for reform even when those plans are adopted by sincere republicans then they are incapable of giving strength and vitality to the political organization to which they belong.

If the democratic party were made up of men who would desert their principles and their policies simply because an honest republican had undertaken to put those principles and policies into effect, it might, in truth, be said that the democratic party is dying.

Commoner, Vol V, pp. 304, 306.

Party Must Espouse Cause of People

"If one would win immortality he must forget himself and devote all his energy towards the advancement of the reforms which he believes to be needed.

The same rule applies to parties. The prudent party that considers only
the chance to win is not nearly so apt to win as the party that devotes itself to a great cause and is willing to suffer if by suffering it can promote
the publice good. If a man can forget himself into immortality, a party can
likewise forget itself into immortality. It is time for the democratic party
to do a little forgetting; it is time for it to put aside, as a controlling
purpose, the thought of getting hold of the offices and dividing the patronage. It is time for it to espouse the cause of the people and to devote itself to this cause without stopping to ask what the effect will be upon the
election. In pursuing such a course it can never meet with dishonorable defeat; and such a course it can never meet with dishonorable defeat; and such
a course is the most likely to lead it to a real victory.

Commoner, Vol IV, p. 415.

A Party for Pioneers

"Ah, my friends,we say not one word against those who live along the
Atlantic Coast, but the hardy pioneers who have braved all the dangers of
the wilderness, who have made the desert to blossom as the rose, the pioneers
who rear their children near to nature's heart, ...where they have erected
school houses for the education of their young, churches where they praise
their Creator, and cemeteries where rest the ashes of their dead -- these
people, we say, are as deserving of the consideration of our party as any
people in this country.

It is for these that we speak. We do not come as aggressors. Our war
is not a war of conquest; we are fighting in defense of our homes, our families, and posterity. We have petitioned and our petitions have been scorn-
ed; we have entreated and entreaties have been disregarded; we have begged
and they have mocked when our calamity came.

We beg no longer, we entreat no more, we petition no more. We defy them."

The First Battle, p. 200.
From Cross of Gold speech at Chicago Convention, 1896.

Careful Selection of Delegates

In order that the democratic party shall remain steadfast, it will be the
duty of every one who believes in the principles set forth in the democratic
national convention to manifest an active interest in the work of organization.
In every precinct throughout the United States democrats should organize.
They should carefully scrutinize the record of every man who aspires to be a
delegate to democratic conventions; and they should see to it that no man is
sent to a democratic convention, county, state or national, who cannot be
depended upon to faithfully represent and defend the opinions of the rank
and file.

Commoner, Vol III, p. 91.

Select Incorruptible Workers

Draw the line, not in anger but in fairness and justice, and see to it that the party organization is clean and incorruptible. Let every aspirant for a position in the party organization be scrutinized. If his present position or his past record is open to objection, let him stand aside. The party has more important work than apoligizing for its representatives, and no representative ought to desire to make himself an issue. . . .

Commoner, Vol VI, p. 241.

Power of Individual Honest Democrats

The contest is on between the many who desire justice and are interested only in good government, and the few who are intrenched behind special privileges and enjoy governmental favoritism. Some who were firm in 1896 have been won over and their places must be taken by stronger and more courageous men. Such an opportunity as is now presented for service to the party may not soon return. One honest, fearless democrat in a precinct can defeat the reorganizers; two in a county can put the corporation element to rout; a half dozen in a state convention can save the party from humiliating surrender.

Commoner, Vol II, p. 142.

Reform More Important than Party

It is more important that reform shall be secured than that those reforms shall come through any particular party.

Commoner, Vol IV, p. 342.

Success Owed to Political Friends

Possibly the reader, if he has never been in politics, may feel that I have devoted too much space to one of my million and a half political friends, but I single him out as illustrative of a very large number from whom I have received so may manifestations of confidence and affection. It is to such as these that I owe the political opportunities which have come to me, opportunities without which it would have been impossible for me to be identified in a large way with great national problems - opportunities by the improvement of which I have been able to accomplish whatever may be placed to my account in the final reckoning.

Memoirs, p. 207.

Party Funds and Bryan

"Bryan receives $5,000 from the state democratic campaign fund for speaking in Missouri. . . "

Now as to the facts: upon invitation of the democratic state committee, Mr. Bryan delivered twenty speeches in Missouri. The subject of compensation was never mentioned. The committee never offered and Mr. Bryan never asked for any compensation. During the trip through Missouri he was asked to send in a statement of his expenses, and he replied that he was interested in the campaign and preferred to contribute his expenses to the campaign fund.

Commoner, Vol II, p. 359,360.

Party Enthusiasm Based on Principle

I cannot believe that the democratic party will throw away the great opportunity it now has to make a successful attack on the strongholds of republicanism, by appealing to the conscience of the country and to the patriotism of the people. We can neither draw honest men to the party nor arouse enthusiasm among our own people by showing a greater desire for "winning" than for principles.

It would be a source of great encouragement to me if in this struggle I felt that I had the active cooperation of all who, like yourselves, have been loyal to the party in recent campaigns. But if I cannot have it I shall console myself with the belief that events will indicate my course and prove to those who have trusted me that in this contest I am only doing my duty as I have tried to do it in preceeding contests."

Commoner, Vol IV, p. 142.

Principle over Patronage

I have hired this hall and I introduce myself because I do not care to speak under the auspices of any club or any organization which is committed to any particular aspirant for office. My concern is not about the name of the personality of the nominee, but about the principles for which the democratic party is to stand. I regard as available all candidates who are in favor of making the democratic party an honest, earnest and courageous exponent of the rights and interest of the masses, and I regard as unavailable all those who are in sympathy with, or obligated to the great corporations that today dominate the policy of the Republican party and seek, through the reorganizers, to dominate the policy of the democratic party.

No democrat is more anxious for the party to succeed than I am. But I do not desire that the party shall win offices only. If that is the only purpose of the party, let its principles be abandoned and let its platform simply declare the party hungry for the patronage.

Commoner, Vol IV, p. 113.

Illinois State Convention Controlled by Reorganizers

The democrats of Illinois might as well face the fact that the state organization is now in the hands of the reorganizers. They controlled the late state convention, dictated the platform and turned the party machinery over to John P. Hopkins. . . .

Those who dominated the convention were themselves so dominated by the great financial interests of the country that they were incapable of representing the people at large.

Commoner, Vol II, p. 207.

Must Oppose Reorganizers

Now we have the delegates selected by the aid of the St. Louis machine working to reorganize the democracy of Missouri and a New York paper speaks regretfully of their failure.

The loyal democrats of the country will learn after a while that the reorganizing idea must be opposed wherever it presents itself whether in precinct, county, state, or nation, for it means the same thing everywhere, namely, the emasculation of the democratic platform.

Commoner, Vol II, pp. 243-244.

Party Must Serve Today

This army, vast and daily vaster growing, begs the party to be its champion in the present conflict. It cannot press its claims 'mid the sounds of revelry'. Its phalanxes do not form in grand parade, nor has it gaudy banners floating on the breeze. Its battle hymn is "Home, Sweet Home," its war cry "equality before the law." To the Democratic party, standing between these two irreconcilable forces, uncertain to which side to turn, and conscious that upon its choice its fate depends, come the words of Israel's second lawgiver: "Choose you this day whom ye will serve." What will the answer be?

Speeches, Vol I, pp. 143-144.

Federal and States Rights

The Democratic party favors the full exercise of the powers of the government for the protection of the rights of the people - each government to act within its constitutional sphere. Our platform demands that federal legislation be added to, not substituted _for_, State legislation.

The predatory corporations have taken advantage of the dual character of our Government and have tried to hide behind State rights when prosecuted in the federal courts, and behind the interstate commerce clause of the constitution when prosecuted in the State courts.

There is no twilight zone between the Nation and the State in which the exploiting interests can take refuge from both. There is no neutral ground where, beyond the jurisdiction of either sovereignty, the plunderers of the public can find a safe retreat.

Speeches, Vol II, p. 184.

Party on Private Monopoly

Here is a plain, candid statement of the party's position. There is no quibbling, no evasion, no ambiguity. A private monopoly is indefensible and intolerable. It is bad - bad in principle, and bad in practice. No apology can be offered for it, and no people should endure it. Our party's position is entirely in harmony with the position of Jefferson. With a knowledge of human nature which few men have equalled and none have surpassed, and with extraordinary foresight, he expressed unalterable opposition to every form of private monopoly. A student of history will find that this subject, and upon other problems of government, the great founder of the Democratic Party took his position upon the side of the whole people, and against those who seek to make a private use of government, or strive to secure special pricileges at the expense of the public.

Because the private monopoly is indefensible and intolerable, the Democratic Party favors its extermination.

Speeches, Vol II, p. 124.

Democratic Party Encourages Honest Work

The Democratic Party is not making war upon the honest acquisition of wealth; it has no desire to discourage economy, industry and thrift. On the contrary, it gives to every citizen the greatest possible stimulus to honest toil when it promises him protection in the enjoyment of the proceeds of his labor. Property rights are most secure when human rights are most respected. Democracy strives for a civilization in which every member of society will share according to his merits. No one has a right to expect from society more than a fair compensation for the services which he renders to society. If he secures more it is at the expense of someone else. It is no injustice to him to prevent his doing an injustice to another. To him who would either through class legislation or in the absence of necessary legislation, trespass upon the rights of another the Democratic party says, "thou shalt not."

Commoner, Vol I, p. 159.

Corporate and Consumer Forces

Today the Democratic party stands between two great forces, each inviting its support. On the one side stand the corporate interests of the nation, its moneyed institutions, its aggregations of wealth and campital, imperious, arrogant, compassionless. . . . They demand that the Democratic party shall become their agent to execute their merciless decrees.

On the other side stands that unnumbered throng which gave a name to the Democratic party and for which it has assumed to speak. Work-worn and dust-begrimed, they make their sad appeal. They hear of average wealth increased on every side and feel the inequality of its distribution. They see an over-production of everything desired because of the underproduction of the ability to buy. . . . Altho the ones who most deserve the fostering care of Government, their cries for help too often beat in vain against the outer walls, while others less deserving find ready access to legislative halls.

Speeches, Vol I, p. 143.

Party Defends Property Rights

The Democratic Party is not the enemy of property or property rights; it is, on the contrary, the best defender of both, because it defends human rights and human rights are the only foundation upon which property and property rights can rest securely. The Democratic Party does not menace a single dollar legitimately accumulated; on the contrary, it insists upon the protection of rich and poor alike in the enjoyment of that which they have honestly earned.

Commoner, p. 137.

Epoch-making Convention

"This is no ordinary occasion. This is an epoch-making Convention. We have had such a struggle as was never seen in politics before. I have been the center of this fight, and I know something of the courage that it has brought forth, and something of the sacrifice that has been required. I know that men working upon the railroad for small wages, with but little laid up for their retiring years, have defied the railroad managers and helped us in this progressive fight at the risk of having their bread and butter taken from them. I have known men engaged in business and carrying loans at banks who have been threatened with bankruptcy if they did not sell their citizenship, and yet I have seen them, defying these men, walk up and vote on the side of the struggling masses against predatory wealth. I have seen lawyers risking their future, alienating men of large business, in order to be the champions of the poor. . . . It seems to me that now, when the hour of triumph comes, the song of victory should be sung by one whose heart has been in the flight."

Memoirs, pp. 518-519.
St. Louis Convention.

CHAPTER

X

POLITICAL LIFE

First Convention

     I formed early the habit of attending national conventions. It so
happened that the Democratic National Convention of 1876 was held in St.
Louis, only seventy miles from my birthplace. My father and mother were
attending the Philadelphia Exposition at the time, but my enthusiasm
reached a point where I decided to go to the convention with some of the
other boys--I do not recall that any of them were as young as myself. I
sold enough corn to secure the small amount necessary, the railroad fare
being only a few dollars and my other expenses being small. I recall that
I stayed all night at East St. Louis, sleeping in a room with more than
thirty others on cots.
     Next day I appeared at the convention hall, but not knowing anyone
from whom I could secure a ticket, I had to content myself with standing
around watching the distinguished Democrats, to me unknown, go in and out
of the convention. But here again my lucky star helped me out. A police-
man, taking pity on me, put me through a window and I had the pleasure of
hearing John Kelly make his famous speech against Tilden. That was my
initiation into national politics. Since that time I have attended every
Democratic National Convention but three, and I was in close touch by wire
with two of the three, those of 1900 and 1908. The Cincinnati Convention
of 1880, therefore, is the only one that I have actually missed since I
was sixteen years old. I was still a college boy in 1880 and Cincinnati
was so far from Salem that I was able to withstand the temptation which
overpowered me four years before.
     When the convention of 1884 was held at Chicago I was living at
Jacksonville, but my income was so meager that I decided that I could not
afford a trip to Chicago, but here again fortune favored me. I was invited
to deliver a Fourth of July address at Greenwood, not many miles from
Jacksonville. In accepting the invitation I answered the inquiry about
compensation by stating that I expected nothing more than my traveling expenses. When I stated the amount, something less than three dollars, he
handed me a twenty-dollar bill with the remark, "That will cover your expenses."
     I was so surprised that I almost forgot to thank him. I decided that
I would construe my good luck as a providential provision for convention
expenses and arranged to go to Chicago.

Memoirs, pp. 97-98.

Admission to Convention

     As it is in all national conventions, it was difficult to get a ticket
of admission. Finding Hon. Telas W. Merritt, of Salem, a prominent politician

at the Illinois headquarters, I asked him if he could secure tickets for Epler and myself. He said he could not secure tickets, but that he knew one of the doorkeepers, whereupon he took us to Joseph Chesterfield Mackin, a Chicago politician, and said in his stammering way-he stuttered- "Joe, pa-pa-pass these b-b-boys in." Joe passed us in and we returned to his door regularly during the sessions of the convention.

Memoirs, p. 98.

Appreciation for Support in Senatorial Contest of 1894

I appreciate more than words can express the cordial good will and the local support of the friends to whom I am indebted for the political honors which I have received. I am especially grateful to those who bear without humiliation the name of the common people, for they have been my friends when others have deserted me. I appreciate also the kind words of many who have been restrained by party ties from giving me their votes. I have been a hired man for four years and, now that the campaign is closed, I may be pardoned for saying that as a public servant I have performed my duty to the best of my ability, and am not ashamed of the record made.

I step from private life into national politics at the bidding of my countrymen; at their bidding I again take my place in the ranks and resume without sorrow the work from which they called me. It is the glory of our institutions that public officials exercise authority by the consent of the governed rather than by divine or hereditary right.

Speeches, Vol I, Intro. XXXVII.

Credo of Commoner

I have twice received at the hands of my party the highest honor it can bestow.

The first nomination came from the delegate in attendance upon three conventions, the second nomination came directly from the voters of the three parties. These honors were bestowed, not because of personal merit, or as a personal compliment, but because of my advocacy of democratic principles.

I am not planning for another presidential nomination--if I were I would not be editing a paper; if I ever become a candidate again it will be because it seems necessary for the advancement of the principles to which I adhere, and that does not now seem probable.

I have no enemies to punish. No matter what a man may have said or done against the ticket in 1896 or in 1900, that man becomes my friend the moment he accepts democratic principles. No matter what a man may have said or done for the ticket in 1896 or in 1900, that man becomes an opponent the minute he turns against democratic principles.

I shall say whatever I think ought to be said, and shall write whatever I think ought to be written. This course may not be popular, but I trust that it will aid in the restoration of Jeffersonian principles.

As a citizen I am interested in saving a good government under which to live; as a father I am interested in leaving a good government to my children. If a good government can be secured it will be reward enough for all that I or anyone else can do.

Commoner, Vol I, p. 116.

Private Citizen Supporting Reforms

I have no plans looking to a renomination at any future time.

I am deeply interested in the reforms for which I have been contending and shall continue to advocate them. I am content to do my work as a private citizen and am sure that I find more pleasure in my present position than I would in the distribution of patronage.

If I ever again become a candidate for the presidency it will be because I am convinced that I can in that way give more effective aid to the cause in which I am enlisted for life, and I am not anxious to be convinced.

I cannot say more without prejudging events.

Commoner, Vol II, p. 272.

Appraisal of Political Situation in 1904

The elections of 1903 are past and the campaign of 1904 is upon us. What shall the democratic party do? Experience has shown that compromises and evasions are as useless from the standpoint of expediency as they are vicious from the standpoint of principle. And, moreover, a defeat which follows evasion and compromise leaves the party weaker for future conflicts, while a fight for principles scatters seed which will bring a harvest later. In 1896 the democratic element in the democratic party, after a fair and honest contest at the primaries, won a decisive victory and obtained control of the party organization. The plutocratic element of the party deserted and ever since that time has been plotting against the party. It threatens defeat if its dictation is resisted and is powerless to give victory when the party yields to its demands. It is planning now to give the democratic nomination to a representative of corporate wealth whose campaign would be made on money furnished by the trusts and whose administration, if won, would be controlled by Wall Street, as Mr. Cleveland's last administration was. To defeat this scheme and keep the party true to the interests of the people will require another contest, but this effort is worth making. In the campaigns of 1896 and 1900 the party had to bear the sins of the Cleveland administration and another surrender would increase the odium and postpone the day of reform. The party must be saved from humiliation and disgrace.

Commoner, Vol III, pp. 322-323.

Plan for 1904

It is now time to organize for 1904. In every state where re-organizers are in control of the party machinery a league should be formed within the party for the avowed purpose of holding the party to its principles. The first should be made at the primaries where the voters speak for themselves. Honest principles should be advanced by honest methods, and the only honest way of settling a question is to leave it to the people themselves. Let the Kansas City platform democrats get together in each precinct and county and form themselves into a league for the defense and propagation of democratic principles.

Commoner, Vol II, p. 382.

Pro Reform, Not Anti-Cleveland

The editor of The Commoner has no personal grievance against Mr. Cleveland, ... But Mr. Bryan is interested in securing reforms, political, economic and social, and being convinced that the Clevelandizing of the democratic organization would mean the abandonment of all prospect or promise of reform, he has felt it his duty to meet Mr. Cleveland's advice with a review of his record and to warn the rank and file against such a disastrous retreat as that counselled by the sage of Princeton.

Commoner, Vol II, p. 411.

Errors of Cleveland

The text of Mr. Cleveland's speech is presented on another page that the readers of The Commoner may know that it sustains the editor's contention that the reorganizers do not want harmony, but control, and that their control means the abandonment of the party's position and a return to the policies and practices of Mr. Cleveland's second administration. He secured his nomination in 1892 by a secret bargain with the financiers; his committee collected from the corporations and spent the largest campaign fund the party ever had; . . .

Having debauched his party he was offended by its effort to reform and gave comfort to the enemy. Virginius killed his daughter to save her chastity; Cleveland stabbed his party to prevent its return to the paths of virtue.

Commoner, Vol II, p. 201.

Individual Opinion

When the campaign of 1900 was over I asked all "Bryan clubs: to drop my name and take some name indicating adhesion to democratic principles, rather than to any person." I stated that my reasons for doing so were, first, that I did not want the clubs to be embarrassed by anything I might do, and second, that I did not want to be embarrassed by anything the clubs might feel called upon to do. Events have justified my fears, and it has sometimes become necessary for me to explain that no person or association is authorized to speak for me, either in endorsing or in opposing any ticket. This applies to all other states as well as to New York. What I desire to say I say for myself, and what I do not say myself, I do not care to have said for me.

Commoner, Vol II, p. 362.

Kept the Faith

Eight years ago a Democratic National Convention placed in my hand a standard of the party and commissioned me as its candidate. Four years later that commission was renewed. I came tonight to this Democratic National Convention to return the commission. You may dispute whether I have fought a good fight; you may dispute whether I have finished my course but you cannot deny that I have kept the faith.

I have always believed, I believe tonight, and I shall ever believe, I hope, that a man's duty to his country is higher than his duty to his party. I hope that men of all parties will have the courage to leave their parties when they believe that to stay with their parties, would injure their country. The success of our government depends upon the independence and the moral courage of its citizens.

Speeches, Vol II, p. 53.

Reason for Defeat

As your candidate I tried to defeat the Republican party. I failed, you say? Yes, I failed. I received a million more votes than any democrat had ever received before, and yet I failed. Why did I fail? Because some who had affiliated with the Democratic party thought my election would be injurious to the country, and they left the party and helped to elect my opponent. That is why I failed. I have no words of criticism for them.

Commoner, Vol IV, p. 290.

For Democratic Principles

I am not coming to present to you any peculiarly Southern doctrine, or a western doctrine, but a democratic doctrine. I am glad that there is a democracy that is as broad as the nation - a democracy that can be proclaimed in any part of the country; and a democracy that is not as broad as the nation is not a democracy that can hope to draw to itself the patriotism and the intelligence of the American people. In 1900 also I was a candidate and the people who then listened to me listened to me as one who aspired to office; but I come to you now, not as a candidate, and yet more interested in the results of the election, more interested in the triumph of democratic principles than I ever was when I was myself a nominee.

I want you to help put the democratic party in a position where it will arouse the conscience of the American people - a conscience which is the most potent power in the world when it is once awakened.

When men tell me that we must surrender our principles; that we must make our party satisfactory to those who do not believe in democracy, or any government of the people, by the people and for the people, I tell them that what we need is not so much to get in men who are not democrats as to drive out of the party those who pretend to be democrats, but whose conduct is a living lie.

I envy my boy because he has one more generation of democracy behind him than I have. But, my friends, the democracy that was taught to me was not the democracy of office holding; it was the democracy of principle, and I want to see my party win a victory by deserving a victory.

I believe we can present these issues and compel the republican party to meet them. All it requires is faith in the triumph of a righteous cause. I come to you, my friends, to appeal to you to maintain the integrity of the democratic party; I come to urge you to do what you can to lift the party to a plane where it can appeal to the conscience of the American people, and challenge discussion of the moral issues involved in all these problems. If I were authorized to frame a prayer for the democratic party - a prayer good enough for any party, it would be: "Oh God, give us faith in the wisdom of doing right."

Commoner, Vol IV, p. 43.

Explanation of "Enemy's Country" Remark

Ladies and Gentlemen: I am very glad to be here tonight - in fact I have lost no opportunity in recent years to make the acquaintance of the people of the east. Something that I said in 1896 was misconstrued, and I have often been reminded that I called this "The enemy's country." After looking at the returns no one can doubt that, in a certain sense, it might be properly so named - but I would not use any term that might seem to indicate that there is any part of this country in which I do not feel at home, or where any theory that I entertain can justly be considered an unfriendly one. I am especially glad to have a chance to speak on occasions of this kind, where those who are assembled may be said to represent the scholarship of a section of the country - the graduates of the great universitites.

Commoner, Vol V, p. 425.

Advice for T. R. Roosevelt

To President Roosevelt: Permit a parting word. You have the contest of your life before you and I desire to render you all the assistance in my power. You have asked congress to enact a law so enlarging the powers of the interstate commerce commission as to permit it to fix and enforce a reasonable freight rate. . . . The railroads will try to persuade you; if they fail in this they will try to scare you; if they fail in this also they will try to defeat your recommendation. It will embarrass you to have strong party leaders against you; you may even be embarrassed by having so many democrats co-operating with you, but you must reconcile yourself to both. In this fight your strength lies in the fact that you have a large majority of the voters of all parties with you.

Commoner, Vol V, pp. 280-281.

Explanation of Attitude on Government Ownership

This statement of my views has been assailed by some as an attempt to force these views upon the Democratic party, and by some as an announcement of an intention to insist upon the incorporation of these views in the next Democratic national platform. Let me answer these two charges. I have tried to make it clear that I expressed my own opinion and I have never sought to compel the acceptance of my opinion by any one else. Reserving the right to do my own thinking, I respect the right of every one else to do his thinking. I have too much respect for the rights of others to ask them to accept any views that I may entertain unless those views commend themselves to them, and I have too much confidence in the independent thought in my own party to expext that any considerable number of Democrats would acknowledge my right to do their thinking for them, even if I were undemocratic enough to assert such a right.

If you ask me whether the question of Government ownership will be an issue in the campaign of 1908, I answer, I do not know. If you ask me whether it ought to be in the platform, I reply, I cannot tell until I know what the Democratic voters think upon the subject. If the Democrats think it ought not to contain such a plank, then such a plank ought not to be included. It rests with the party to make the platform, and individuals can only advise.

I am now prepared to confess to you that it has been received more favorably than I expected. It has not been treated as harshly as I thought possible it would be treated. That it would be greatly discussed by others I hoped. There is this, however, that I do expect, namely, that those Democrats opposed to Government ownership will accompany their declaration against it with the assertion that they will favor Government ownership whenever they are convinced that the country must choose between Government ownership of the roads and railroad ownership of the Government. I cannot conceive how a Democrat can declare, no matter to what extent the railroads carry their interference with politics and their corruption of officials, he is still opposed to Government ownership.

Speeches, Vol II, pp. 93-95.

Acceptance of 1908 Nomination

There is a Divine law of rewards. When the Creator gave us the earth, with its fruitful soil, the sunshine with its warmth, and the rains with their moisture, He proclaimed, as clearly as if His voice had thundered from the clouds, "Go work, and according to your industry and your intelligence, so shall be your reward." Only where might has overthrown, cunning undermined or government suspended this law, has a different law prevailed. To conform the Government to this law ought to be the ambition of the statesman; and no party can have a higher mission than to make it a reality wherever governments can ligitimately operate.

Recognizing that I am indebted for my nomination to the rank and file of our party, and that my election must come, if it comes at all, from the unpurchased and unpurchasable suffrages of the American people, I promise, if entrusted with the responsibilities of this high office, to concentrate whatever ability I have to the one purpose of making this, in fact, a government in which the people rule - a government which will do justice to all, and offer to every one the highest possible stimulus to great and persistent effort, by assuring to each the enjoyment of his just share of the proceeds of his toil, no matter in what part of the vineyard he labors, or to what occupation, progession or calling he devoted himself.

Speeches, Vol II, pp. 118-119.

Credo of Democratic Party

The democratic party, if it is to be a power for good in this country, must be the defender of human rights. It must devote itself to the protection of human right. It must declare, establish and defend the true relation between man and property, a relation recognized by both Jefferson and Lincoln - a relation which puts man first and his possessions afterwards; a relation which makes man the master of that which he has created, a relation which puts the spiritual and moral life of the nation above its material wealth and resources. This is the great struggle of today and it is a struggle in which the democratic party must take an important part.

Go into the orchards and see the seed or the grafted twig into a great tree whose leaves furnish shade and whose fruit gives nourishment to man. Measure if you can the mighty forces behind the grain and the tree, and know ye that the forces behind the truth are as irresistible and as consistently at work. God would have been unkind, indeed, had he made such ample provisions for the needs of man's body and less adequate provision for the triumph of those moral forces which means more to the race than food or clothing or shelter. He is a political Atheist who doubts the triumph of the right. He lacks faith in the purposes and the plans of God who for a moment falters in the great struggle between truth and error - between man and mammon.

Commoner, Vol IV, p. 277.

CHAPTER

XI

FRIENDS' APPRAISALS

His Wife

Early Charity

When he was a pale, slender youth of twenty, he came to visit in my
home. I asked my father's permission to take him to the station in my
phaeton. At the foot of a particularly bad hill there was a man trying
to repair a broken harness. Mr. Bryan said, "Wait a minute. I had better
help that man." I said, "Don't bother with him. I know the family. They
are shiftless. You would only waste your time." We drove on a little way,
but he was uneasy. "Stop, please, I must go back. He needs my help," he
said. He went back and while he repaired the dilapidated harness, the all
too short hours of our visit passed.

This might serve as an epitome of his life - "I must go back. He
needs my help."

Memoirs, p. 298.

Discovery of Power as Speaker

An epoch in his career as a speaker came at the age of twenty-seven,
shortly after we went to Nebraska. He had spoken in a town in the western
part of the state, came home on a night train, and arrived at daybreak.
I was sleeping when he came in, and he awakened me. Sitting on the edge
of the bed, he began: "Mary, I have had a strange experience. Last night
I found that I had power over the audience. I could move them as I chose.
I have more than usual power as a speaker. I know it. God grant I may use
it wisely." And as it was his custom all through life to carry to his
Heavenly Father any new development, he prayed.

This was the beginning of that power which was his - explain it as
you like. I speak positively of his power, for I have seen proof. For
years I attended political meetings. Social functions might be crowded
out, but political meetings went on forever, and from the platform I saw
it all. If conditions were favorable, his mood was transmitted to his
listeners. He smiled, and the smile rippled away over his audience; he
frowned, and so did they; he grew tense with emotion, they bent forward
and sat upon the very edge of the seats.

Nor was the power over an audience shown only in these moods. An
unusual instance may be cited at a meeting in the summer following the
campaign of 1896. Mr. Bryan spoke in a little Utah mining town. The
surrounding mountains were so high that the valley in early afternoon was
already in shadow. He spoke from the second-story balcony of the railway
station to a great audience of miners with mine lamps on their caps. Mr.

Bryan had just suffered a defeat. He was speaking to them after an unsuccessful struggle. But his youth and his deep earnestness rang to his audience on every clear note of his voice. While he was speaking, the shadows had deepened. It was twilight when he closed his speech with the statement that "all his life, whether in victory or defeat, he would fight the battles of the common people. His life was pledged to their cause through all the years to come."

With closing phrase, there came the moment when applause conventionally follows, but none came. There was a deep silence, and one miner after another took off his cap, until that great crowd was standing with bared and bowed heads. His mood of consecration had carried to them.

After a tense pause such a roar of cheers filled the valley as sent echoes rattling back from the hills; a clamor of applause.

Memoirs, p. 248-250.

Man of Principle

Whenever a new political issue arose, Mr. Bryan and I always discussed it fully, and the following was a typical conversation:

The Wife: "But isn't that an extreme position? The question is new. People don't understand too well. If you stand for that, they will call you a fanatic, a wild-eyed reformer, and a few other choice things."

Mr. Bryan: "But I must stand there. Don't you see, my dear, that a leader must be well in advance. All progress comes through compromise; not a compromise of principle, but an adjustment between the more radical and the less radical positions. If I begin far in advance, when the compromise is made, our position will be much ahead of the place I would have secured by a less advanced standpoint."

The Wife" "Do be more moderate. I cannot bear to have you so abused."

Mr. Bryan: "Don't mind about me. These questions are more important than my personal fortunes."

And he would take the extreme stand, submitting to misunderstanding and ridicule for the sake of the compromise which would be most advantageous to the cause.

Memoirs, p. 299.

Life of Service

But although he was keen-minded in his observation of political forces, he always hesitated to turn them to his personal advantage. After the first election of Wilson and before his selection of his Cabinet, Mr. Bryan was dining with warm friends in Richmond, Virginia. One of the gentlemen said in the course of the conversation: "Mr. Bryan, I want to see you President of the United States, and therefore I hope that if Mr. Wilson should offer you a place in his Cabinet, you will decline, because your presence in his official family will be an embarassment to you in seeking the next nomination." Mr. Bryan paused for a moment and then said with great feeling: "My friend, I am not wise enough to know what is best for my political future. But of one thing I am certain, and that is, if Mr. Wilson invites me into his Cabinet, and I think I can be of service to the country, it will be my duty to serve." And then he added impressively, "Whosoever will save his life shall lose it."

Memoirs, p. 300.

Simplicity of Taste

With a generous spirit was combined an almost ascetic self-denial, or perhaps we had better say an extreme simplicity of taste. His needs were few. If he had a box of particularly fine handkerchiefs with cleverly embroidered autographs, he was pleased, but speedily lost them. When his stock ran low, he purchased anything anywhere, and was equally content with a bit of cotton hemmed on a sewing machine. He had no rings. He wore no scarf pin. Shoes were made to order and of the best leather, but simple and always the same style. His string tie and turn-down collar, his alpaca coat, became a part of himself.

Though he was so simple in his tastes, he found the greatest pleasure in any evidence of affection. A gift of an apple, a picture, a cane - no matter how small - would touch his emotions. The gift which he prized most of all was a watch given him by members of the Department of State at the time of his resignation. The amount given by each was small (twenty-five cents), with the result that everyone from the assistant secretary to the youngest messenger bore a part. He wore this watch until his death and showed it to friends with the greatest pride, as no other Secretary of State had received a similar tribute of affection.

Memoirs, p. 302.

Chautauqua Speaker

Upon the Chautauqua platform Mr. Bryan was always perfectly at home. He met the perpetual heat, the restlessness of the great throngs which usually overspread the adjoining grove, with genial ease and command. His leisurely approach, his humanity and humor soon won the audiences and continued to hold them to the end.

Mr. Bryan usually spoke at length fortified by the ever present pitcher of ice water. His message was so simple, so passionate, so keyed to lofty issues, it never failed to find an eager response.

Memoirs, p. 286.

Bryan Listened to Mind of America

But Chautauqua is something deeper than concerts or inspirational lectures. It is more than the gathering together of great crowds in the interest of civic progress.

When Mr. Bryan stood in the Chautauqua tent at night under the electric lights and the starlight, with practically every adult and most of the children from miles around within sound of his voice, he could forget the hardships and weariness of travel. His voice would grow deep and solemn, for he knew he was speaking to the heart of America.

It is not too much to say that Mr. Bryan has remained the most popular Chautauqua lecturer in this country for thirty years. Each year when he returned from his tours he had not only spoken to, but had listened to, the mind of America. He had had an opportunity to know what America was thinking and he had helped America to make up her mind.

Memoirs, pp. 287-288.

Lectures to Students

During these years Mr. Bryan delivered a series of James Sprunt lectures at the Union Theological Seminary at Richmond, Va. These lectures were nine in number and were published by the faculty under the title "In His Image." This week spent in the Theological Seminary was a very happy one. He spoke several times of the joy it gave him to speak connectedly upon such themes to a body of students, and expressed a hope that if he lived to be old, he might arrange lectures at a series of colleges, and "you can go with me and meet these pleasant friends," he said.

One can only condense the work of these busy years. He addressed the Legislatures of West Virginia, of Kentucky, and of Florida. He spoke to the students at the State University of Florida, at Brown University, at Dartmouth, at Phillips Brooks House in Harvard. He lectured at the Moody Bible Institute, at the Bible Institute of Los Angeles, California, at the Lane Theological Seminary in Cincinnati, at Winona Lake Bible Conference, at Carnegie Hall, at the Presbyterian General Assembly, at the Miami Bible Conference, at the National Christian Endeavor Convention. He made a campaign of Flordia to raise an endowment fund for the State University at Gainesville, spent one summer on the Chautauqua platform, campaigned the State of Florida for election as delegate-at-large to the National Democratic Convention in New York, speaking in the county seat of each of Florida's sixty-six counties, making the journey by automobile, coming home tanned by the sun and bright-eyed, full of happiness because he was beginning to know people all over the state, and found them such "fine fellows."

Memoirs, p. 474.

His Income

Mr. Bryan's income is derived from his lectures and his pen, and he had time enough left to devote nearly two months of this year to campaign speeches and for these speeches he not only receives no pay, but for the most part he pays his own expenses and does not ride on passes either. He is interested in the reforms which he advocates and is glad to aid the men who are fighting for these reforms. During the past six years he has given more than nineteen thousand dollars to various campaign committees, besides devoting a considerable portion of each year to political speeches delivered without compensation in different part of the country.

Commoner, Vol II, pp. 360-361.

Political Awakening

His father's congressional campaign in 1872 was his first political awakening, and from that time on he always cherished the thought of entering public life. His idea was to first win a reputation and secure a competency at the bar, but he seized the unexpected opportunity which came to him in 1890.

Life and Speeches, p. 25.

Always a Democrat

Mr. Bryan never at any time or place denied his political affiliation with the democratic party or permitted it to be questioned. His parents were democrats before him, and he counted himself a democrat in his youth because his parents were, and after he was grown, was a democrat because of his belief in democratic principles and policies. He made democratic speeches in 1880, before he was old enough to vote, and has made democratic speeches in every campaign since. He has attended democratic conventions for about twenty years, and has never been a delegate to a convention of any other party.

Commoner, Vol III, pp. 230-231.

Foreign Hosts

India

The arrival in Bombay yesterday of Mr. William Jennings Bryan, the leader of the great Democratic party of the United States is an event of singular interest. Mr. Bryan needs no introduction to the citizens of Bombay. His fame is already world wide.

The issues of American politics are no direct concern of Bombay; it is enough for this city to know that Mr. Bryan is one of the greatest living Americans to make it glad to have him in its midst.

Long before the time for the meeting to commence - 6:00 - the town hall was packed. It is estimated that with those standing by the windows and doors, there were 3,000 persons present, and of these only a small portion were seated, the side and the back of the hall being filled with people perfectly willing to put up with the discomforts of standing. His address was on the Prince of Peace.

Mr.Bryan spoke for exactly one hour, and throughout the whole of his oration he had the undivided attention of his audience. Those who are best calculated to know affirm that the company last night was the largest ever gathered within the town hall, and it consisted of diverse races and creeds. It consequently speaks much for the magnetic influence of the man when it is remembered that for one hour, Mr. Bryan held this gathering under the spell of his eloquence, while he discoursed on a subject in which at least two thirds of those present could have but little, of any, sympathy

(The lecture was his religious lecture, entitled "The Prince of Peace." His style never loses its deeply impressive character, and one feels that the man is giving vent to feelings right from the heart.

Commoner, Vol IV, p. 65.
(From an editorial in the Times
of Bombay, India, March 27, 1905.)

Japan

I welcome you, first of all, as the representative of one of the most friendly and most sympathetic nations in the world; I welcome you again as a strong link in the chain of friendship existing between your country and ours; I welcome you once more as one of the foremost statesmen of the age. Furthermore, I welcome you as one who possesses the divine gift of winged words, bestowed only upon the elect. Lastly, I welcome you, sir, as a man, fearless and unflinching in the fight for what he holds to be right. May your stay be long, pleasant and agreeable to you, sir.

Commoner, Vol IV, p. 20.
(From the welcoming speech of the
mayor at Kagoshima, Japan,
October 31, 1905.)

Japan

We have recently been busy receiving distinguished foreign guests who have visited our country. These distinguished guests were received properly by us. At the same time they no doubt left several good influences upon our social and spiritual life.

But no one equals Mr. Bryan, who left more instructive lessons during his one week stay in the capital. He is a great man whom we have revered for a long time as a leader of the democratic party of the United States as a great orator and as a candidate for the presidency of the country. Having an interview with him, and having observed his conduct and listening to his speeches, our reverence towards him increased more and more.

He is a man of principle. He insisted upon the importance of an ennobling ideal of political parties in each country, and expressed his desire for the promotion of justice, not only among individuals, but also among nations.

In the presence of the governor, of the mayor, and members of the Tokyo city he gave lessons that the officers of the city must be responsible, temperate and faithful to the practice of justice. May heavenly blessing be upon the great man and his family during their long voyaging travel. May his instruction given to our countrymen bear fruit, and produce such a great personality as he is, among our own people.

Commoner, Vol IV, p. 28.
(From the Shinjin, Tokyo newspaper.)

Philippines

Bryan. This is a name among names. Others may boast of it but in their cases it does not mean so much. The daily press today fills column after column regarding him as his name is in the mouth of everyone.

In fact few names of Americans can be mentioned among Philippinos which will excite more feeling. Bryan did not need to come here in order to be popular.

The principal impression produced by his presence, even upon his adversaries in politics, is his constant ability and discretion.

Bryan has made no statements or passed any judgment regarding the Philippine administration. He has not given any excuse for his being characterized as an agitator, or a scoffer at the enterprise which the United States as a nation, has undertaken in these islands.

Commoner, Vol IV, p. 36.
(From a Manila newspaper,
December 27, 1905.)

Hawaii

The country sees in him a man who believes in a "Square Deal" as firmly as does president Roosevelt; a man who loves his fellowman; a man with a fine spirit, a large heart, a nature simple and serene; a man who, with firmness and enthusiasm stands fearless, calm, insistent - sometimes almost alone in opposing the policy or traditions of his party, when such opposition seems to him right; a man who accepts defeat in such a spirit that it seems like victory.

Commoner, Vol IV, p. 3.
(From a commercial advertising Newspaper at Honolulu.)

Twenty-First Birthday

As I reread the letters of our rather lengthy courtship (four years) I find his diversions to have been Sunday school, church, prayer meeting, an occasional church social, and at long intervals, a circus or an evening at the theater. I select a letter written on his twenty-first birthday, beginning -

"Have just signed a fictitious name, 'Lazarus,' to my essay Pauperism and learned my Sunday-school lesson for tomorrow, and now, though it is nearly eleven P.M., am going to write to you. . . .

The day (my twenty-first birthday) has been spent very quietly; took a glance over my boyhood, at its pleasures gone beyond recall, at its few successes, its few sorrows. Then full of gratitude for the blessings of the past, I turned, with some trembling, to contemplate the unknown future, its responsibilities, its possible successes, and its probable misfortunes. I would dread to be compelled to set forth upon this sea with nothing but the light of my reason to aid me. What a blessing it is that we have that guide, the Bible. The future looks bright. I have almost graduated and will be prepared for work. I have good health, good friends, and best of all, a loving, faithful sweetheart."

Memoirs, p. 450.

Blessings

When I was in law school, I was fortunate enough, as I was in my college days, to fall under the influence of men of ideals who helped to shape my course; and when but a young man, not out of college yet, I was guided to the selection of one who, for twenty-four years, has been my faithful helpmate. No presidential victory could have brought her to me, and no defeat can take her from me. I have been blessed with a family. Our children are with us to make glad the declining years of their mother and myself. When you first knew me, they called me, in derision, "The Boy Orator of the Platte." I have outlived that title, and my grandchildren are now growing up about me. I repeat, that I have been fortunate, indeed. I have been abundantly rewarded for what little I have been able to do, and my ambition isnot so much to hold any office, however great, as it is to know my duty and to do it, whether in public life or as a private citizen.

Speeches, Vol II, pp. 416-417.

Scholar

The scholar must be something more than a mental machine; he must be something more than an expert calculator; he must be something more than a shrewd and successful business man.

Commoner, Vol V, p. 434.

Last Campaign Speech

If, on the other hand, the election shall be against me, I can feel that I have left nothing undone that I could have done to bring success to my cause. And I shall find private life so full of joy that I shall not miss the presidency.

Speeches, Vol II, pp. 416-417.
(Closing speech of campaign,
November 2, 1908.)

Glory for Few in Politics

In politics as in the army, the generals receive the glory while the enlisted men die in the trenches. The names that are prominent become household words, while the multitude who bear the burden are nameless in history.

Memoirs, preface to p. 10.

Grateful Appreciation

No one has been the recipient of as large a measure of unselfish devotion; no one is in better position to record with grateful appreciation the kindness received.....

And yet, while during the six years and three months of my official life I was practically powerless to reward those who had contributed to my success, I am sure that no one in this country - probably no one who ever lived - has had more friends, kept them for a longer period or received from them greater loyalty or more constant support. I have reason to know that the masses are patriotic and incorruptible. They cannot be purchased and they cannot be terrified. No matter how they may err or be led astray, the American people are sound at heart. They have solved successfully all problems that confronted them during the momentous years of our nation's history and there is not the slightest reason to doubt that they will meet every emergency, rise to every responsibility and prove that their capacity for self-government is an undeniable as their right to self-government.

Memoirs, preface pp. 11, 12.

Those find truth who seek for it - who seek not casually or carelessly, but earnestly and constantly. The best evidence that one can give of his faith in a truth is to be willing to suffer for it. Christ gave utterance to a principle of wide application when He said, "He that findeth his life shall lose it, and he who loses his life for my sake shall find it." So it may be said of truth. He whose only object is to save his own political life will lose it, and will deserve to lose it, but he who is willing to lose his life for the sake of a cause or a principle, triumphs with the cause or principle to which he adheres; he grows with it and enjoys the confidence of those who are wedded to it.

Commoner, Vol III, p. 153.

APPENDIX

A

BRYAN AS ORATOR

By permission of Dorrance and Company, Philadelphia, Pa. this excerpt from Charles F. Horner's Strike the Tents is included because it is so personally revealing of Bryan's character and manner.

From 1909 until he passed from earthly scenes, I had a considerable part in his lecture plans, and since I made countless engagements for him, I am sure of the truth of what I write.

One of the first lectures which Bryan delivered on my circuit was at Blue Rapids, Kansas. Since that was forty-five years ago, I am sure my friends in that lovely little city will not mind my saying the population was them about fifteen hundred people. Of these, a thousand, young and old, had season tickets. The tent could not contain even half of the Bryan audience, which did not matter at all because thousands could sit or recline on the grass under the trees, and all hear very well. I think we charged twenty-five cents for admission, and as I remember, the cash receipts were about a thousand dollars. Therefore, we had sold four thousand single admission tickets which, with the season ticketholders, if they were all present, made an audience of five thousand people. . . .

Seldom, indeed, could he enjoy a few minutes of quiet without interruption. Word of his presence would spread through the train and there was an almost constant stream of curious but friendly people up and down the aisle, and most of them must shake hands with him. The greetings from the men who filed past scarcely varied: "Mr. Bryan, I voted for you three times and I just want to shake your hand." I often wondered how he could have failed in the elections since all the people we saw had supported him.

Somehow, probably by rural telephone or word of mouth, news of his journey had been spread about and at every train stop we would hear the shouts of the crowd assembled at the station. Regardless of the import of letter, telegram, or editorial, he would go to the platform to greet his admirers. There was no good for me to protest. He said the people perhaps had made trouble for themselves to come and he would not disappoint them. That was true, I know, because some of them had left their fields or shops and maybe traveled miles to have a fleeting glimpse of the Great Commoner, and possibly grasp his hand for an instant and say they had voted for him three times. Too often the train would begin to move along before all could get within reach.

When we reached a temporary destination, there was really acclaim. As the train slowed to a stop, we could see flags and banners, and the music of a bankd would reach our ears. When Mr. Bryan appeared, shouts, steam whistles and automobile horns rent the air. The mayor and committee were on hand and behind them were troops of boy scouts, flocks of flower girls and badge-bedecked school chilren were herded together by their monitors. Beyond all was the throng of people who crowded the station platform. There is something quite disconcerting and even a bit frightening in the effort of an ordinary person to force a path through a crowd of human beings facing him. Conveying Bryan through a little sea of friendly faces lit by shining eyes was like the passage of the hosts of Israel as they walked between the walls of parted water of the Red Sea. I have thought often of such an experience, repeated for me perhaps hundreds of times. One caught in the grip of a multitude of fellow being, say in Times Square or Madison Square Garden, or even in a great political campaign, can scarcely escape a sense of the spirit of the mob, and fear the crush in the movement sweeping from the composite mind of an unordered multitude.

I could feel, but even now I cannot describe the difference in the concourse that welcomed Bryan day by day. Surely they did not come because of curiousity. Most of the citizens of our section had seen him before, perhaps often. Many, maybe nearly all, had heard his voice. There was no play of the emotions generated in the heat of a political campaign. No radios were blaring his name or words. The great newspapers of the nation were not presently printing black headlines in praise or fault. True, Bryan was known by more and had been seen by more people than any other human being in the world. Here he came, a simple private citizen engaged in the labor of earning his daily bread.

Even though his welcome by multitudes was ever genuine and kind, I was often puzzled by the quality of it. There was shouting and applause, but neither was tumultuous or vociferent. I could detect no evidence of pent-up feelings or surge of passion such as characterize a political campaign. No lurid advertising had evoked curiosity or sown seeds of unwarranted expectation. But there they were, the unnumbered multitudes from the farms and villages, the cities and railroad yards. I could have wished that they might all have been crowded into the Chautauqua grounds because Mr. Bryan was met by more people without than within. But why were they there, everywhere he went? He was then enacting no crusader's role and bore no promise of political reform. He was merely going from place to place to stand under hot canvas and talk to people about "The Prince of Peace" or "The Value of an Ideal."

Later, at exactly the appointed moment, we would escort him quietly into the tent from the rear so that only a few people could see him enter. All the hard seats were filled, and around the edge of the open canvas cover people would stand, ten, twenty, or thirty persons deep. When Mr. Bryan was introduced the audience would clap their hands, some of them would shout, and down in Texas there would issue a wave of rebel yells. Once again, I was puzzled with the subdued gentleness even in the warmest applause. I have been in embassy gatherings and meetings in affairs of state and have been told that the modest hand clapping was an evidence of the good taste of those present. No doubt that is true, but if that was an expression of taste and breeding, so was this. Or was this something that came from a deeper recess in human hearts? Bryan would stand with a smile on his face, with a fan in his hand, doing nothing, acting nothing, to prolong the expression of welcome. In a moment or two he would raise his arm, the palm of his hand turned to the people, and a quiet would come like the fall of a rose leaf on the grass.

In July, 1925, I rode, as an honorary pallbearer, in the sad cortege that followed W. J. Bryan's catafalque from the New York Avenue Presbyterian Church in Washington to Arlington Cemetery. With me were two former members of President Wilson's cabinet, a well-known United States Senator, a Congressman, and another former official in the Wilson administration. They were talking, of course, of our departed friend. One spoke of that gesture, hand raised high with the palm turned towards the people. A gesture that had brought an expectant calm to a multitude a thousand times and more. It was, they agreed, nothing less than majestic. I had seen that raised arm, ah, hundreds of times. It was, at once, a command and a benediction, and it seemed to transmit a feeling of peace.

Again and again, I placed myself so that I could look into the faces of the people as he spoke. I could sense and see the evidence of their emotions, but no sound from it would reach my ears. For an hour and a half I thought they were enjoying a deep feeling of peace and even happiness. Most of them, I suppose usually carried in their hearts the same kind of worries and fears that perplex men in all places and stations. Here, for a little while, these would slip away from their consciousness and they could reach towards the stars.

Was all of this caused by the stirring power of great oratory? Not exactly. Those people were silent, except that now and then a wave of applause would sweep across the tent, or a smile would expand into a ripple of laughter, but both would fall into silence as abruptly as the sound of them had burst. They were almost motionless, too. I saw no nudging of elbows nor a glance aside into a neighbor's eyes, or even a shift of weight from one tired foot to another among those who stood. Certainly they did not appear to be chained to the spot, but all of them, with strong bodies or weak ones, clothed in good raiment or covered by the garments of labor and the farm, seemed almost literally to float on a placid plane. I think what I am trying to say is that physical sensations seemed to be suspended for a time. Perhaps the poise and calm of the speaker had something to do with it. Whatever motion there was in him was like the rhythm of a mountain stream flowing through the rocks. He scarcely moved on his feet. One hand held a palm leaf fan which was never still. The other rested alternately on a block of ice in a basin on the table, and then on top of his head upon which the heat beat down pitilessly. Even his frequent gestures seemed to be extensions of those motions. Water would stream down his face for he had the hottest place in an acre of discomfort, but he, too, seemed unaware of fatigue or heat.

I do not know to what extent those people had enshrined Bryan as an ideal in their thoughts, if at all. I have tried to discover for myself the reason or reasons for the phenomenon I witnessed so many times, and I think I found three. They may be only theories but they are the only explanations I can find to add to the undoubted perfection of the greatest orator I have ever heard. First, those people may have sensed in Bryan a greatness of spirit that perhaps escaped those who were never present on a like occasion. Second, they heard the voice of a man they esteemed expressing in clear words the best fruit of their own meditations and the very peak of their aspirations even though these were usually hidden within themselves. Finally, if we can accept at all the proposition that the affection which one man bears for another is reciprocated by the latter, that proposition may furnish part of the explanation. Bryan loved people and had a faith in them that was sublime. He believed that if they could and would act and think according to their best instincts, that altogether they possessed a power that could move and save the world. Perhaps, after all, the enraptured state of mind of the Chautauqua audience reflected the stirring of power within its composite heart. Perhaps a similar awakening may explain why a mighty unity of the force of hand and will could

win a global war in 1945. I think there is but one word that can correctly
define the feeling of the Chautauqua audience for Mr. Bryan. There was respect,
of course, admiration and even affection. But over all there was one quality
which seemed never to be absent, and that was reverence.

I do not see how anyone who did not hear Bryan speak could have a concept
of the force of his words. . . . The quality of the sound that flowed from
his lips enhanced the value of the words. He would emphasize by letting his voic
fall a little as though there was a period following the accented word, or he
would affect the same result by raising the tone. His sentences were clear-cut
and never confused in arrangement. They were accurately keyed and there was
little or no transposition from the key when he reached a climax. The tonal
quality of his voice surpassed that of any other speaker or speakers I have
ever heard. Every syllable was uttered so distinctly that no one need cup a
hand behind his ear to hear its full import.

If his audience numbered a thousand people or ten thousand, there could
be no one in it who could not hear distinctly. Once or twice, on a quiet summer
evening I have stood at a distance of a block away and even then I could hear
what he said. His tones would never swell to a shout nor break into a roar.
When the volume expanded in a climactic phrase, there was nc loss in the fullness
and music of the tone. Along with the melody of his voice and grace of his gestures, the flash of his eyes would seem to reach even to those who sat far away.

There was method in all of this as there was design in what he said. He
told me that he always tried to speak in a way that would require of the people
the least possible mental and physical exertion to understand what he said and
thus they could use their minds without interference to understand what he
meant. That is the reason he did nor perplex them with unfamiliar words. Many
would say that his voice would "carry" farther than that of anyone else. That
was foolish, he thought. In a given volume of sound one voice would carry as
far as any other. The reason he could be heard at a great distance was because
he enunciated every syllable clearly and distinctly and would not permit the
sound of one word to crowd into the tone of another.

I was well inured to travel, but when I kept up with Bryan for a couple of
weeks, I was exhausted, and I didn't need to make the speeches. On some particularly difficult days he was tired but with a few hours, and sometimes a few
moments of sleep, traces of fatigue would disappear. He would drop into slumber
in a moment, in a train coach or with his head resting on the back of a seat in
an automobile. When he finished an address, thousands of people would press
forward to shake hands. He would sit on the edge of the platform and grasp the
hands of all comers, using his left hand as well as his right. When he had
been surrounded by throngs at the stations or in the hotels, and I would suggest that we should find, somehow, a few minutes for relaxation, and delay his
appearance a bit, he would say that he could relax better when he was speaking.
He is the only person I ever knew who could rest physically while he was making
a speech and that was because his mental and body functions were so well coor-
dinated.

pp. 105-131

APPENDIX

B

MEMORIAL ADDRESS
BY
WILLIAM JENNINGS BRYAN JR.

On March 19, 1960 William Jennings Bryan, Jr. delivered this address at the Nebraska Centennial in Lincoln.

I am grateful to you all, for the privilege of taking part in these proceedings, and joining in this tribute to the memory of William Jennings Bryan, for he was truly a great and good man.

He first came into political prominence when the people of this Congressional District chose him as their representative in Congress, in 1890, and 1892 and for thirty-five years thereafter he was a power in the political and social life of this country, although only in six of those years did he hold public office.

He lived in an age before radio and television were known, when the only means of reaching the public was by face to face contact, or by the medium of the press.

As he seldom had the support of a majority of the press, his political crusades were mainly carried on by voice, in direct contact with the people. Year in and year out, he toured the country on the Chautauqua, lyceum and lecture circuits, in order to earn the funds that enabled him to carry on an unending battle for the principles and reforms he felt were necessary, to protect the rights and liberties of the common people. For this reason, he probably met personally and spoke directly to more of the American people than any other man of his time.

His impact upon people was altogether unique. His dynamic personality, his clarion voice, and his ability to express his thoughts in simple. graphic words, compelled the attention of friend and foe alike. No one could be indifferent about him; indeed there was no middle ground for those who heard him. He was either regarded as a dangerous radical, and was ridiculed, or feared and hated as a menace to society, or he was regarded as an inspired prophet and crusader for the salvation of his fellow man.

He had in his personality an indefinable something, that bound people to him, with a feeling much deeper than mere admiration or regard. It was an enduring bond of personal love and affection, that is rarely found in public or private life.

Your fellow citizen, Mr. Bryan, was a man of many parts. Others will speak of his power as an orator, and of his achievements as a crusader for political and social reforms; but to me, the most remarkable quality that Mr. Bryan possesed was the ability to inspire in a multitude of followers the same faith and personal devotion that he felt for his fellowman. They found in his personality and character, a rare combination of qualities that are universally admired.

And so, Madam Chairman, with your permission I shall use my allotted time to speak of some of the traits of character that, in my humble opinion, made your fellow Nebraskan the appealing, magnetic personality that he was, in both public and private life.

Certainly one of the foremost of these qualities was an utter sincerity of purpose that governed his every act. It was a quality indelibly impressed upon family and friends, and countless numbers of his contemporaries who have spoken of his public life.

Perhaps their statements were best epitomized by President Franklin D. Roosevelt, at the dedication of the memorial statue which stands in Potomac Park, in Washington, D. C., when he said: "As we who were his friends and associates in the Wilson administration look back on those days, I think that we would choose the word "sincerity" as fitting him most of all. It was that sincerity which brought him the millions of devoted followers; it was that sincerity which served him so well in his lifelong fight against sham and privilege and wrong. It was that sincerity which made him a force for good in his own generation and has kept alive many of the ancient faiths on which we are building today."

In a message of condolence to my mother, at the time of his death, President Cooledge expressed the same thought when he said: "He has been a leader in the advocacy of many moral reforms and was the representative of the efforts for purity in our political life.....The sincerity of his motives was beyond dispute.....It would be difficult to find among his contemporaries anyone with so large a circle of friends who had so generously bestowed upon him their esteem and confidence."

But tonight, I want to speak of him not as a public figure, but rather of his private life. To those in the inner circle of friends and family, there was no mystery about this quality of his personality. They knew that sincerity, and honesty, were basic principles of his whole philosophy of life, and that he simply could not be otherwise.

He instinctively turned to prayer in his hours of trial or indecision. His was a faith that took firm hold of the promise of Divine guidance, and which felt in the assurance of Divine approval, an armour and sword, against which no foe could stand.

He believed in the persuasive power of example. In his lecture, "The Fruits of the Tree", he said: "Example is the means of propagating truth. It is a slow process this winning of converts by example, but it is the sure way. A speech may be disputed, and even a sermon may not convince, but no one has yet lived who could answer a Christian life. It is the unanswerable argument in support of the Christian religion."

To one with such upbringing and personal philosophy every question, whether public or private, had a right or a wrong side.

Mr. Bryan's only concern was to determine the right, and in this determination his sense of responsibility to God, dictated by his own conscience, was his only guide. Once he determined where the right lay, he adhered to his belief with all the zeal of a crusader.

Political expediency never controlled him. He loved his friends and gave consideration to their views, but he was adamant against any suggestion that for personal or political advantage, he soft pedal here or be silent ther He never counted the odds against him for he would cheerfully accept defeat rather than surrender a principle.

You will remember too, that in all his fights, indeed throughout all his political life, Governor Charles W. Bryan, or "C. W." as he was affectionately known, was Mr. Bryan's confidant and closest political adviser. His counsel was sought on all political matters and yet, even "C. W." could not influence his brother, when it came to a matter of principle.

Recently, in going through a mass of their correspondence, I again and again found letters that disclosed wide differences of opinion on political policy and procedure. These were not statements made for public consumption, but the frank private expressions of brother to brother.

Prior to the 1912 Convention at Baltimore, Maryland, when Mr. Bryan was urging the leading candidates to demand a progressive Chairman of the Convention, he writes: "Dear Brother: I am sorry my course is not entirely satisfactory to you, but I am doing the best I can. I shall not attempt to dictate a candidate. I am going to do what I think best for the country and the party. I hope it will not be a disadvantage to the paper, but my obligation to both country and party requires me to put them first."

And again he writes, "Dear Brother, I am glad you have given your opinion fully and I agree with most you say. But in case of uncertainties, I 'walk by faith' and do what I think best and take the consequences."

On his return from a trip around the world, Mr. Bryan made a statement on government ownership of railroads that was widely criticized as being a "socialistic" idea. Governor Bryan, smarting under this criticism, apparently disapproved of the statement, for we find this letter written in January, 1907: "Dear Brother: I am sorry you do not like the plan. I urged it first in 1904 and again when I returned from the around the world trip. It may as you say be rejected as impractical, but I have not in the past been deterred by fear of unpopularity, from advocating what I believe to be good, and I shall not begin now."

These letters and many others deal mostly with political matters, but Mr. Bryan's dedication to his Christian ideals was even more abundantly revealed, in the quiet reaches of his private life.

I am eternally grateful for our thirty-six years of close association that took me with him through political campaigns and on his travels in foreign lands.

I like to believe that I was taken along because he really wanted me with him, but it has been intimated by some of my relatives, that in the early days at least, I was so full of mischief that he simply did not dare to leave me at home. Whatever the reason was, it gave me an opportunity to share with him countless memorable events of his remarkable life.

I have stood with him in his hours of political triumph and in hours of political defeat; I have been with him when he addressed parliaments and the heads of state, and when he spoke to a handful of children in a foreign mission school. I have heard him preach a great sermon in some metropolitan church and when, standing alone with bowed head, he gave thanks to his maker, in the silent cathedral of a giant redwood grove.

I have seen him under strain and fatigue from weeks on the road, and in rare moments of relaxation when he returned to his home and could assemble his family around him.

I, therefore, can testify of my own knowledge and experience that under any and all conditions of physical and emotional life, and more than any person I have ever known, he consistently lived according to his beliefs.

It was a continuing marvel to me that all through the years, I never knew him to wilfully do an unkind act, or engage in malicious or personal criticism of any person. I never once heard him enter into an angry argument or utter any cruel or bitter words.

He did not believe in swearing, so no one ever heard him utter a profane word. In the book of memoirs, Mrs. Bryan quotes an entry in the journal she kept of their life in Washington, as follows: "I wanted to go to the Senate when the cabinet members were confirmed but could not get away. I did go to the State Department and see Will sworn in as Secretary. I told him I had never heard him swear before, and was interested to know how he would do it."

He did not smoke, although there was a brief time in his first campaign, when in order to be a regular fellow at stag affairs, he would occasionally light a cigar and pretend he was smoking it. However, I cured him of this practice before it became a habit; and honesty compels me to admit that was the only contribution I was ever able to make to better his behavior.

During the 1896 campaign, some admirer in the Philippine Islands, sent him a case of Manila cigars that were hermitically sealed in glass tubes. They were a constant challenge to me, so one day I took one out behind the barn and showed my admiring gang how a cigar really should be smoked. A short time later, my mother found me lying there on the ground, unable to lift my head, and carried me into the house. When my father returned that night, he sat on the foot of my bed and gave me a lecture I will never forget. He pictured the evils of smoking in a way that was both eloquent and convincing. By the time that he finished, I was all through with smoking, but he had me really worried about himself. After a short pause, I said: "But Daddy, then why do you smoke?" He gave me a startled look, but his answer came without hesitation: "My boy, I meant every word that I said, and I shouldn't smoke either. I will never touch tobacco again as long as I live." And, in fact, he never did.

He believed that intoxicating liquor was a curse to humanity and, of course, he never took a drink himself. He even refused to serve it at official functions when he was Secretary of State.

Mr. Bryan was a kindly man. He could not see need or misfortune in any form without wanting to do something about it, and the wish was always followed by action.

The problems of youth were his special concern and he never missed an opportunity to speak to students, whether in the grade schools, or high schools, or colleges. Some of the finest talks that he ever made were addressed to such groups.

"The Fruits of the Tree"; "The Value of an Ideal"; and other lectures, were inspired by his desire to help students. Always he sought to persuade the young to link their destiny to a high ideal. He pleaded with parents to assist their children, admonishing them in these words: "Give a child food and he will hunger again; give him clothing and his clothing will wear out; but give him a high ideal and that ideal will be with him through every waking hour, lifting him to a higher plane of life and giving a broader conception of his relations to his fellows."

In our family circle, he implanted his high ideals, mainly by his silent example. He was always ready and anxious to give his children the benefit of his experience, but never sought to force his opinions upon us.

Of course, there were occasions when we required a sound spanking, because of some activities that were less than ideal, but such unpleasantness he usually left to Mrs. Bryan.

Some of his letters, written at milestones in my life, such as my graduation from college, my admission to the Bar, or my first appointment to government service, are priceless examples of a father's devotion; never seeking to dictate or control my decisions, but redolent of his philosophy of life.

I believe it was about the time I graduated from college he wrote me a wonderful letter regarding the choice of a life's work. After discussing the opportunities in various fields, he closed with these observations: "I would be glad to see you excel in public speaking, but it is more important that you shall be good, than that you should be brilliant; most important that you shall be right, than that you should be eloquent. If the responsibilities of office fall upon you, remember that public office is a public trust, and that a good name is rather to be chosen than great riches, and loving favor rather than silver and gold."

He once planned to visit me at a time when I was faced with some particularly difficult decisions. The following is so typical of his attitude, I want to quote from his letter: "I am looking forward to September when we shall be able to have some long talks together. I do not want to advise you except as you may desire, but I shall be glad to counsel with you whenever you need the wisdom that comes with age, and I shall support you fully wherever you have to act on your own judgment."

No one will ever know the number of his benefactions, but I do know that for many years they were a matter of real concern to my mother, who had to disburse the family living expenses. However, she used to say: "He gets so much pleasure giving his money away - I just can't scold him too hard."

In our own country he endowed many small libraries; in dozens of schools established prizes for the best essay during the year on the science of government, and in scores of others, scholarships for the education of youth.

On his trip around the world, Mr. Bryan founded scholarships for the education of native children in the mission schools in many foreign lands. I find among his letters a memorandum addressed to his brother in 1906, listing the scholarships he had established at Pekin and Nankin, China; Rangoon, Burma; at Allahabad, India; Luxor, Egypt; Beirut, Syria; and at Jerusalem. There is also correspondence showing that years later these scholarship funds were still being sent.

Mr. Bryan was a family man. He longed for the day when his labors would permit him to remain at home and enjoy a normal family life. That, however, was a day that never came. Always and forever there were, somewhere, issues that had to be met; battles that had to be fought; some group or cause that needed his help; and he went where duty called him.

As the years went by, we heard more and more plaintive protests such as the following: "I am getting old but as far as I know, I am perfectly well. If I did not have to 'save the country' so often, I would be able to be with my family more." And again I quote from his letters: "Give my love to all the kin and tell them that I am looking forward to a few days of leisure before I die, when I will have time to live up to the obligations to my relatives. The public has had a first mortgage on me during most of my life."

It was a marvel to all of us, how faithfully he did live up to his family obligations. In the days of his travel, there were no dictaphones or tape recorders to help him, and his voluminous mail was answered by hand. Yet, somehow, no family anniversary or holiday greetings escaped his attention. I saw to it that we children remembered.

Mr. Bryan's tolerance for the opinions of others was another quality that bound his friends to him. His condemnation of what he believed to be wrong was not personal - it was righteous indignation against the act. He never consciously permitted himself to hold bitterness against those who opposed him.

Thus we find him admonishing one of the relatives : "At any rate, remember that family relationships should not be disturbed by differences of opinion on political matters. Each should do what he thinks is right and be charitable towards those who do not agree with him."

During the course of the Scopes trial in Tennessee, he received a particularly bitter and critical letter from an old Colorado friend, who resented his taking part in the case. It was the sort of letter that most of us would have promptly consigned to the waste basket, but Mr. Bryan's reply was typically tolerant. He wrote: "Dear Mr. _____, I am not able to terminate our long friendship as cheerfully as you do and I shall not allow a difference of opinion on religion blot out the pleasant memory of earlier days.....I am glad however that something deters you from appearing in the Tennessee case. I only wish it were something less serious than advancing years.

He was often criticized and sometimes ridiculed and maligned, but the common people knew their own.

They believed him an inspired leader who asked little for himself save an opportunity to serve. They knew him as a true and courageous champion, who fought for every reform he felt necessary to restore the powers of government to the people's hands; to safeguard their liberties and insure their equality under the law.

INDEX

Ability, Use All of One's   54
Advice from General John C. Black   29
Ages of Man   13
Ancestors, Value of Good   4
America, Bryan Listened to Mind of   114
American Civilization   51
American Destiny   51
America Strong in Ideas and Acts   79
America, World Looks to   79
Appraisal of Political Situation in 1904   104
Appreciation for Support in Senatorial Contest of 1894   103
Arbitration, Advantages to   89
Arbitration Good for Society   64
Arbitration Must Include Senate   89
Arbitration, Plan for   88
Arbitration   Practical   76
Arbitration Through Equal Rights   64
Arbitration Would Reduce War to Minimum   89
Authority by Consent of Governed   50
Ballot Avoids Dam of Public Opinion   47
Banks' Ills, Corrections for   67
Bible, Influence of   23
Boers, Avoid Joining England Opposing   85
  Help Liberty-Loving People   87
  Supported Fight for Independence   86
  Sympathy Based on Principles   86
Bryan, Mary
  Early Charity   111
Bryan, Silas
  Public Life   2
  Religious Attitude   2
Bryan, Silas Lillard, Early Work and Education   1
Bryan, William Jennings
  Acceptance of 1908 Nomination   109
  Admission to Convention   102
  Advice for T. R. Roosevelt   108
  Always a Democrat   115
  Basis, Political Philosophy   6
  Blessings   119
  Chautauqua Speaker   113
  College Courses   27
  Disclaims Possible Second Term   70
  Effect of Mother on Character   3
  Explanation of Attitude on Government Ownership   108
  Explanation of "Enemy's Country" Remark   107
  Father's Beliefs of Sources of Happiness   4
  Father's Religious Influence on   2
  First Convention   102
  For Democratic Principles   107

For Home Industry 78
His Income 115
Kept the Faith 106
Last Campaign Speech 120
Lectures to Students 114
Opposed Second Term for Himself 70
Pro Reform, Not Anti-Cleveland 105
Scholar 120
Simplicity of Taste 113
Twenty-First Birthday 119
Success owed to Political Friends 97
Tariff Bill 78
Business, New Era of 66
Businessman, Broad Definition of 66
Character, Good 10
Character, Slow Creation of 14
Character, Power of 14
Citizenship, All Share 53
Citizen Important, Every 41
Class Privilege, No 53
Cleveland, Errors of 105
Colonialism, Defeats Self-Government 84
Colonialism and Republic Antagonistic 82
Common Man, Highest Title 41
Common People, Cultured Oppose 44
Common People, Praise for 41
Common People Strength of County 43
Common Right and Divine Right 48
Competition, Not Trusts 58
Conscience and Heart 48
Conscience, Power of 14
Conservation of Resources, Support for 67
Convention, Epoch-making 101
Corporate and Consumer Forces 101
Corporate vs Natural Man 57
Corporations, Protection Against 58
Corruption Preverted Government 56
Court Injunction, Opposed to 55
Corporal Punishment, Value of 22
Creation, Mystery of 19
Creation, Study of 33
Creator in Silence 33
Credo of Commoner 103
Credo of Democratic Party 109
Cross of Gold 72
Defeat, Reason for 106
Democratic Party
Careful Selection of Delegates 96
Democrats Must Support Principles Above Party 95
Democrats Should Avoid Republican Methods 95
Defends Property Rights 101

    Encourages Honest Word   100
    Enthuriasm Based on Principle   98
    Funds and Bryan   98
    Morality of   93
    Must Espouse Cause of People   95
    Must Avoid Temporary Success   93
    Must Serve Today   99
    Position of   93
    Power of Individual Honest Democrats   97
    Principles of   93
    Private Monopoly   100
    Reform More Important than Party   97
    Select Incorruptible Workers   97
Death God's Way   38
Decisions Based on Moral Principle   6
Declamation Contest   28
Demagogue or Statesman   16, 47
Democracy and Aristocracy   42
Democrat and Aristocrat   92
Democracy
    Conducive to Highest Civilization   43
    Founded on Brotherhood of Man   40
    Heart over Plutocracy of Wealth, of   57
    Is the Common People   40
    Perpetual   42
    People, Mirror of the   15
    Spreading   49
    Strength of   39
    Voice of the People   50
    World Power   49
Depositor, Protection for   65
Destiny Argument Invalid   80
Die for Rights of Others   17
Difference Between Man and Brute   13
Direct Vote, Advantages of   69
Education, Prizes for   27
Education and Service, Value of   12
Employer, Employee, and Society have Equal Responsibility   77
Equality Great Issue of Day   53
Equal Rights   63
Evil, Beginning of   15
Faith   17
Faith Generates Achievement   18
Faith in Democratic Ideas   18
Faith Necessary to Accept Materialism   35
Faith in Ourselves and Mankind   17
Family Home   22
Father's Advice   26

Federal and States Rights	99
Financial Accounting	26
Food for Body, Mind and Heart	19
Fifty-Third Congress Avoided One-Term Resolution	70
Filipinos, Majority of Americans for	84
Fortune, Child of	20
Free Speech	17
Geneology	1
Giving to Others	9
Glory for Few in Politics	120
God and the Election	37
God, Belief in	33
God in a Watermelon	36
Gold, Decide For or Against	72
Government by Injunction, Opposed to	64
Government Monopoly over Private Monopoly	50
Government, Opposing Forces of	39
Government, Opposing Forms of	81
Government Ownership	61
Government, The Unfinished Form of	42
Grateful Appreciation	120
Greatest Good for Greatest Number	49
Greed, Awakening Against	60
Hawaii	117
Heart Over Mind	10
Ideal Destiny of America	81
Ideal, Highest	8
Ideal Should be Unattainable	9
Ideal, The Value of an	7
Ideals Freer than Merchandise	75
Ideals, Need for	7
Ideals, One's Influences Others	8
Idle Rich, No Place for	54
Illinois State Convention Controlled by Reorganizers	99
Immortality	36
Imperialism Extended in Philippines, South Africa and Cuba	82
Imperialism Ignored in World	85
Imperialism Injures Reputation	84
Imperialism Not Destiny	80
Imperialism Un-Christian	81
Inalienable Rights, All Races have	74
Income Tax, America Worth 2%	68
Income Tax, False Economy of Opponents of	68
India	115
British Responsible if Indians Cannot Govern Themselves	87
British Rule in India Despotic	87
Indian Education, Taxes Not Used Appropriately for	88
Indians, Appreciation of Bryan from	88
Individual Opinion	106
International Education	91

445

Investigation Board	90
Japan	116
Jefferson Confident of Triumph of Truth	45
Jefferson Cultured and Common Man	44
Jefferson on Political Parties	92
Jennings, Mariah Elizabeth	3
Jury Law, Amend	54
Labor,	62
Dignity of	63
Rights of	63
Laborer in Europe, Progress of	62
Laborer Owes Society	76
Laborers Owe Respect for Law	77
Lessons, First	22
Liberty, Land of	46
Liberty, Right to Fight for	79
Life of Service	112
Life, Origin of	34
Love over War	38
Loving Heart, Effect of	10
Majority and Minority	49
Majority, Rule of	40
Man a Part of All, Each	14
Man Can Answer Moral Question, Average	46
Man of Principle	112
Man, Rights of	39
Man, What is?	12
Miracles	34
Morality Paramount in Government	16
Moral Sense in Politics	6
Nations, Duties of Superior	73
Nations' Strength in Principle	75
Natural Rights of All	62
Natural Rights vs Corporate Rights	60
Netherlands adjusting Colonial System	82
Officials, No Gifts to	55
One-Term Consititutional Amendment, Resolution for	69
Parents Religious Flexibility	25
Party for Pioneers, A	96
Patience	19
Peace, Heroes of	46
Peace of Mind	20
Peoples Similar, All	91
People Purify Politics	55
Philippines	117
Physical Moderation	12
Plan for 1904	105
Plutocracy, Against	57
Political Awakening	115
Political Corruption	56

Politics and Protective Tariff   75
Power of Primaries   95
Power of Wealth, Remedy   61
Politics, Purity in   56
President Jackson Reduced Bank Power   66
Principle over Patronage   98
Private Monopoly: Indefensible   58
Principles, Importance of   6
Privileges, No Special   56
Prize Money   30
Public Opinion, Essence of Moulding   30
Public Service, Need Unselfish   55
Public Speaking, Essentials of   31
Public Speaking Training   28
Races, Superior and Inferior   72
Radical and Conservative Necessary   48
Reason not Force   90
Reason over Force   80
Reform, Discontent Precedes   47
Reforms Interrelated   64
Reforms, Private Citizen Supporting   104
Religious, Association with Many   37
Religious Environment, Importance of   25
Religious Tolerance   37
Religious Training and Conversion   24
Reorganizers, Must Oppose   99
Resurrection   36
Right over Expediency   94
School Record   23
Scopes Trial   35
Serve, All Classes May   8
Service Repays Debt to Ancestors   7
Service, Value of Great   9
Sherman Act, Opposed to Repeal of   65
Spanish-American War   83
Spanish-American War must not be War of Conquest   83
Speak to the Heart   31
Speaker, Theme more Important than   31
Speaker, Discovery of Power as   111
Speaking, Early   23
Sppech Introduction   30
Student, Lifelong   11
Suffrage, Political Value of   71
Superior Race Must Act for Self-Preservation   74
Tariff Disproportionate Tax   68
Tariff Law Catches Little Fish, not Big Ones   78
Tariff, Reduction of   77
Tax, Need Equally Based   76
Title, Cannot Buy People with   84
Trusts, Creeping   59

Trusts, Encroachments of   59
Trusts, Rockefeller on   59
Trusts, Tendencies of   60
Truth in the Bible   20
Truth Omnipotent   21
Truth, Regard for   24
Truths, Self-Evident   44
Vice-President Should be Informed   70
Voters Should Control Party   94
Wealth Created by Laborers   61
Woman's Suffrage   71